Crash Course in Teen Services

Donna P. Miller

Crash Course

LIBRARIES
U N L I M I T E D
A Member of the Greenwood Publishing Group

Westport, Connecticut • London

Library of Congress Cataloging-in-Publication Data

Miller, Donna P., 1948–
    Crash course in teen services / Donna P. Miller.
        p. cm. — (Crash course)
    Includes bibliographical references and index.
    ISBN 978–1–59158–565–7 (alk. paper)
    1. Libraries and teenagers—United States.   2. Young adults'
libraries—United States. I. Title.
    Z718.5.M55 2008
    027.62'6—dc22   2007032758

British Library Cataloguing in Publication Data is available.

Library of Congress Catalog Card Number: 2007032758
ISBN-13: 978–1–59158–565–7

First published in 2008

Libraries Unlimited, 88 Post Road West, Westport, CT 06881
A Member of the Greenwood Publishing Group, Inc.
www.lu.com

Printed in the United States of America

The paper used in this book complies with the
Permanent Paper Standard issued by the National
Information Standards Organization (Z39.48–1984).

10   9   8   7   6   5   4   3   2   1

CONTENTS

INTRODUCTION

FOR WHOM IS THIS BOOK WRITTEN?

This book is written for those public library staff members who are new to the profession, have had little or no formal training, or both, in addition to those who may be experienced in the public library field but want to learn new techniques and information in order to update their practice. Those librarians who provide training for new staff or volunteers will also benefit from reading this book. The book deals specifically with library services and programs designed to meet the needs of teens, and the information included will be relevant for library staff members who serve that group of customers. Note: the author will use the term "customers" rather than the more formal term "patrons" to describe the people who patronize the library by checking out or using resources or taking advantage of programs delivered or sponsored by the library. For the purposes of this book, the terms "teens" and "teenagers" will be used interchangeably and will refer to youth from 13 through 19 years of age.

WHY SERVE TEENS?

Those who work in public libraries, especially small libraries that may have only one staff member, often find themselves performing a myriad of functions and serving a wide variety of customers. One of the most challenging yet important customer groups of public libraries is teens. The U.S. Census Bureau reported in *Census 2000* that 14.48 percent of the population in the United States is in the 10- to 19-year-old age bracket (U.S. Census Bureau 2001). According to Michael Cox, a public library staff member in Pueblo, Colorado, children aged 0 to 18 represent 20 to 32 percent of the population of the United States (Cox 2006). From this data, it appears that this younger segment of the population in our country is growing. Obviously, not all of these youth are teens, but those who are not yet teens will soon become members of this age group. This group could represent a significant percentage of the customer base for the public library. Therefore, it is important to the success of the library that public library staff members learn how to serve this group effectively, efficiently, and in a way that results in our teens developing a positive impression of libraries.

Not only is providing excellent customer service to teens important to the health and well-being of public libraries, but it also has ramifications for our communities and even our entire country. Well-informed and well-educated teens can positively impact the ongoing health and prosperity of our society. These soon-to-be adults will either be the citizens who will recognize that libraries do indeed serve the common good, or they will be among those who neither value nor support public libraries. The experiences that they have as teens when they visit and use the public library may well be the determining factor as to which attitude this group of citizens adopts. Thus, public library librarians and staff have an obligation to provide exemplary service to these customers. Not only is this the right thing to do, but it is also the prudent thing to do, to help to mold young citizens and preserve our public libraries.

WHAT YOU WILL FIND IN THIS BOOK

Readers will find essential information on a variety of topics throughout this book. The topics included are those that have been identified by the author as ones that are foundational to operating a public library serving teens. While the book does not provide exhaustive coverage of every topic, it is intended to include the most critical points of information, to help library staff members who are looking for strategies and techniques that can be immediately implemented as needs occur. Thus, the purpose of this book is to give readers a practical, usable handbook to assist them in serving teens. The book has been written with the practitioner in mind, so the information is intended to be of a practical nature, and the strategies included can be implemented easily without additional information. A brief description of the contents of each chapter follows.

Chapter 1, "The World of Today's Teens," provides an overview of teen culture including teens' peer groups, the issues that they face in contemporary society, some of the popular teen icons, and strategies for relating to teens in a way that brings success. Due to the fact that some factual information and background is necessary for this chapter, the reader will find references to the work of a few social scientists and specialists in the area of teen brain research. The succeeding chapters will not include many references, as this book is primarily based on the experiences and opinions of the author.

In chapter 2, "Reality Reference: Assume Nothing," the author includes tips for being more approachable to teens, a model for the reference interview to help staff gather information from teen customers, some examples of reference interviews, information about virtual reference services, suggestions for working with teachers and school library staff, guidance on identifying and dealing with plagiarism, an explanation of the Big6 research model, and a list of "tips and tricks" to use when working at the reference desk.

Chapter 3, "The Teen Collection," is a thorough guide for building and maintaining a collection of materials, in various formats, to serve the needs and reading interests of teens. The chapter covers essential information on each part of the collection development process, from describing what is involved in developing a collection policy to describing an array of electronic resources that are available for either free use or purchase.

Readers' Advisory can be an important service to encourage teens to use the library, and chapter 4 will introduce this service to readers, along with specific strategies for implementation, interviewing techniques, and bibliotherapy, instructions for conducting book talks with teens, a discussion of genres of fiction and types of nonfiction books, and a listing of several resources to use. In addition to the material included in this book, Libraries Unlimited is developing a comprehensive database on its Web site that will present a wide variety of tools that can be accessed and used by library staff for Readers' Advisory and other services.

Chapter 5, "Programming for Teens," describes various types of programs for teens that can be implemented in the library. Included are such programs as book clubs (both traditional and online), summer reading programs, school visits to promote the library, and a variety of other in-house programs for teens. Since evaluation of programs is important to help library staff continue to improve their offerings, tips and tools for evaluating library programs are offered.

Not only must library staff have an understanding of today's teens and their world, but also they must then follow up by creating a teen space in the library that welcomes teens and helps to make them feel comfortable in the library. Chapter 6, "Creating a Teen-Friendly Library," addresses this important topic. Although smaller libraries may not have space to set up an actual teen library, it is possible to create a cozy area for teens that is unique to their needs. This chapter will discuss how to provide this type of space.

Library staff will discover that it is not enough to meet the needs of teens in the present, but that instead, for the library to continue to be used by teens, staff must keep up with teen-related interests, services, and topics, as well as continuing to promote the library to these young customers. Chapter 7, "The Three Ps," addresses the critical topics of professional resources, professional growth, and public relations to help library staff maintain a teen-friendly library that continues to serve the needs and high expectations of the teen customer.

HOW TO USE THIS BOOK

The book is organized so that specific sections can be used at the point of need. Therefore, it need not be read from cover to cover. Instead, readers can review specific chapters or sections of the book to find pertinent information on a specific topic. In addition to the table of contents and the index, "plain English" terms will be used throughout the book, or, in cases where it may be necessary to use library jargon, these terms will be explained to the reader. Also included is a bibliography listing books, articles, and other resources. Lists of pertinent free Web resources are included at the end of each chapter. All of these resources will provide readers with further information on various topics. Finally, lists of book awards, celebrations, projects, and organizations are included to give readers additional resources for implementing programs and projects for teens. As indicated previously, readers can also find more comprehensive information on many of the topics covered in this book at Libraries Unlimited's Web site, which will be updated regularly.

CHAPTER 1

The World of Today's Teens

WHO ARE THESE STRANGE CREATURES?

We've all been teens, yet once we reach a certain stage of adulthood, we seem to be unable to remember what it was like to be younger. Thus, we sometimes struggle to understand or relate to these gangly or graceful, loud or quiet, brash or thoughtful, loving or hating, happy or sad, trendy or traditional, funny or humorless, pack-animal or isolationist (sometimes all within a matter of moments, it seems) people called teens or teenagers. As librarians, we are committed to organizing and providing information and recreational reading resources for all of our customers, but despite our best efforts, it can seem that we are not successfully communicating with this group, nor are we serving their needs. Although there are many complex reasons for this, some facts are easy to understand, and if librarians will take a bit of time to learn these facts, their encounters with teens in the library will be much more pleasant. Further, one would hope that if the teens that frequent the library have positive experiences, they will not only be return customers, but they will also tell their friends that the library is a safe, enjoyable place to visit.

Of course, the first and most difficult challenge is to attract teenagers to the public library in the first place. Chapter 5 will address this challenge by suggesting programs and services appropriate for teens. For now, we will assume that we do have teens visiting our libraries. So how can we better understand and communicate with them?

The first important point is that we need to understand the physiological changes that impact teens' behavior. We know that teens' bodies are growing and changing rapidly, and this can account for their physical discomfort when they try to adjust their bodies to fit into chairs, use computers that may not be at a comfortable height for them, or access materials on shelves either too high or too low for their reach. Chapter 6 will address the physical environment needed for teen areas. But what accounts for the often erratic behavior we see in teens, and how can library staff deal with it in a way that is satisfactory to both the teen customer and the library staff? Knowing a bit about current brain research on teens will certainly help!

Researchers in the past believed that tremendous brain growth occurred from birth to about age three, and from that age on, our brains grew at a much slower rate of speed. Scientists such as Dr. Jay Giedd of the National Institute of Mental Health have recently conducted studies suggesting that another period of rapid brain growth occurs at puberty in an area of the brain called the frontal cortex (Public Broadcasting System 2002). This part of the brain, which controls decision making, planning, and impulses, is not only changing rapidly during adolescence, but it is also the last section of our brains to stabilize. Thus, it is easy to understand why teens are emotionally volatile and impulsive, and make poor decisions at times.

If librarians take into account the physical factors and brain issues impacting teens, it will be much easier to deal with them in a way that shows understanding rather than judgment. Teen librarian Michele Gorman says that we can "Think of teen reference as an opportunity...to act as a surrogate frontal lobe—stepping in to help with planning, processing information, and problem solving" (2006, 34). What a healthy and positive approach to a struggling teen this could be! If we as library staff can operate from a more objective, adult perspective when interacting with teens, taking into account what we know about physical challenges and brain development, interchanges with teenagers in our libraries can be much more positive.

TEEN CULTURE

All we need do to realize that today's teens live in a very different world from those of us who are over 30 is to watch these folks closely. We can quickly see that today's teenagers are "wired for sound" as well as for sight and touch. The pervasiveness of such small technological devices as PDAs, cell phones, MP3 players, portable DVD players, notebook computers, and other items is amazing, and today's teens are not only the primary purchasers and users of such items, but they are also the experts in setting up and troubleshooting almost any technology-based piece of equipment that is available. The long-term cultural impact of our teens being so tech dependent is unknown, but one immediately noticeable effect is that teens are definitely multitaskers.

This means they are not only adept at performing more than one task at a time, but they actually seem to demand that a multitude of devices should be available and that they should have the opportunity to perform two or more tasks simultaneously. The author has personally witnessed students walking down a hallway, visiting with friends while they text message and listen to music on their MP3 players.

In addition to being hardware savvy, today's teens use various software applications and are frequent visitors to a variety of Internet-based resource sites. In fact, computer use, especially the use of Internet resources, is a daily fact of life for many teens. According to a *Newsweek* cover story, written over five years ago, profiling teenagers in the United States, 48 percent of teens who were polled reported that they used computers at home on an almost daily basis (Begley et al. 2000, 55). One would suspect that this percentage has increased over the last five years as computer hardware has continued to decrease in price and increase in availability. Due to the pervasiveness of technology and the commonplace family situation in which, if two parents are still residing in the home, both probably have jobs outside the home, today's teens may actually spend more time alone than previous generations. Although they certainly still "travel in packs" and are very peer oriented, when today's teenagers are away from their friends, they tend to be by themselves, without adult supervision, in their own world of the Web and video games (Begley et al. 2000, 54). Thus some teens prefer to work alone, with very little supervision or support from adults.

Power of Peers

The term "peer pressure" is almost a cliché when used to describe the super dependent relationships that today's youth have with their friends. At no time is peer pressure more powerful than in adolescence. It seems contradictory that while teens are struggling to become independent, they are at the same time tightly bonded to their friends. Perhaps part of the tight bonding and group orientation we see in today's teens are a direct result of the fact that many are spending so much time alone at home. Thus, they need peer group support now more than ever. In fact, the previous generation of teens has carried this team orientation into the workplace, so that huge corporations such as Microsoft have implemented a flattened organizational model in which work teams are responsible for all decisions about and implementation of the projects they are assigned. The good news here is that today's teens better understand how to be team players, and, in fact, they can often accomplish more within a group than they accomplish alone. So what does this mean in terms of the public library?

Library staff members need to be tolerant of teens working in groups and realize that the quiet library and traditional "shushing" librarians must be things of the past! Productive noise is now the norm, so librarians must not only be accepting of the increased noise level but must learn to work with groups of teens rather than expecting to deal with only one person at a time. This situation can be uncomfortable and feel a bit threatening, but if the librarian can work within this context with teens and even support and help facilitate the research and information seeking that groups are engaged in, he/she will establish a very positive rapport with the young adult customers. Some tips for interacting with groups of teenagers are provided below:

- Greet groups of teens in a positive, pleasant manner as they enter the library.
- If a group of teens appears to be having success, leave them alone!
- If you see that a group of teens needs help, approach them confidently, but in a friendly, open manner.
- Try to ascertain who the group's leader is, and direct questions to that person.
- Accept that the library may not be quiet when teens are working in groups.
- Unless a group of teens is obviously disturbing others, allow them to talk and interact as needed to accomplish their task.
- Be open to groups of teens coming into the library just to "hang out."

Teen Issues

Today's teens live in a much more complex world than many of us who grew up in the 1950s or 1960s. They face and deal with issues that we could not have even conceived of in our teen years. Some of the issues with which we may be familiar are much more prevalent in today's society than they were when we were teens. While we may have known about some of these issues, they may not have personally touched our lives, or, if they did, their severity was perhaps less than is experienced by today's teens. Some teen issues that librarians need to be aware of, as they may have implications for interactions with teens, as well as providing librarians with a list of topics for collection development, are listed below.

In her book *Helping Teens Cope: Resources for School Library Media Specialists,* Dr. Jami Biles Jones includes the following young adult issues (Jones 2003, iii, iv):

- Maltreatment: neglect and abuse
- Substance abuse
- Depression and suicide
- Eating disorders and problems with body image
- Self-inflicted violence
- Divorce
- Teen pregnancy
- Relationship violence
- Driving
- Bullying and cliques

In addition to the issues previously listed, the author would suggest that the following are also pertinent issues for today's teens: body piercing and tattoos, social group identification (for example, as Goths, Punks, Techies, Band O's, Populars, Crunchies, Boarders, Jocks, Ropers, Emos, Preppies, etc.), peer status, racial and ethnic discrimination, sleep deprivation, media influence, extended family relationships, images in popular culture, socioeconomic level, sexual identity and homosexuality, and others.

Teen Language

Just as trends, fashion, and fads for teens change with the seasons, so too does their slang. Although it is helpful to know what "bad," for example, really means to today's teens, librarians may find that they cannot stay abreast of the most current teen isms. Thus, librarians are faced with three possible choices: (1) as a library staff member, you can find a young adult with whom you have a good relationship and ask her to tell you what the newest terminology is; (2) you can continue using the slang that was in vogue yesterday and hope that it's still viable; or (3) you can avoid using slang altogether. The third choice is truly the most appropriate, as trying to sound "hip," "cool," "with it," or whatever else to show that you are informed and in control may instead make you sound stilted and desperate to be accepted. Unless you can pull off the use of teen slang (and you should know whether or not you can!), simply resort to "plain English" when talking to teens. Teen librarians may become friends with those customers they serve, but they will never be members of a teen's peer group. Thus, it is more professional and safer to use Standard English, particularly in a reference interview in which the librarian is soliciting information that is critical if the teen is to be able to access and use the library's resources effectively and efficiently. For more information on young adult language and slang, see the Web sites listed in the Web Resources section at the end of this chapter.

WHAT'S HOT AND WHAT'S NOT

Just as young adult slang changes rapidly, so too do the cultural icons, technology, literature, movies, and other items that young adults embrace or, conversely, reject. However, although they do not need to keep up with and use young adult slang, librarians DO need to know at least some of the information resources, literature, entertainment venues, and technology that teens embrace, as they will have an impact on such things as the young adult collection (both print and nonprint), the technology that should be available in the library, the computer software applications to purchase, and the Web sites that teens use frequently. If young adults visit the library and cannot find the latest young adult (YA) novel on the state award list, or discover that they cannot use their laptop because the library has no wireless drops, or are told that "We don't allow people to access their personal email accounts in the library," or ask the librarian whether they can download an audio book to their MP3 player and are informed that the library does not have downloadable audio books, chances are that the library has just lost customers. In fact, due to the strong peer group connections that most teens have, the library will probably lose a multitude of young adult customers due to one negative experience such as any of those mentioned previously. So, how does a librarian keep up with what's hot and what's not? Some suggestions are provided below.

It is of primary importance that librarians incorporate technology into their own lives. Paula Brehm-Heeger (2006) suggests that teen librarians can do this by buying a new desktop or laptop computer on which to create and use an instant message account, start a personal blog, utilize RSS and Atom feeds, explore teen social sites such as *MySpace™,* buy or borrow an MP3™ player or iPod™ and download books or music, and take digital photos and upload them to a photo-sharing site such as Flickr™. One note: social networking sites such as *MySpace* are receiving substantial criticism today due to the potential for pedophiles to use the sites to obtain information about youth that enables them to contact young people whom they intend to victimize. Thus, librarians may not want to actually set up a profile on a site but instead just browse the site to gain a better understanding of the topics and issues of interest to teens.

Brehm-Heeger also suggests that teen librarians learn to play video games and join teens in Dance Dance Revolution™ (or DDR) (2006, 46). However, performing DDR, like speaking slang to teens, could be quite risky unless the librarian is truly coordinated and can look "cool" while engaging in this rigorous activity! Additionally, the space and money needed to purchase the equipment for DDR and video games may be cost prohibitive if library budgets are small. It is sufficient just to know about DDR to have a better understanding of one of the popular activities in which today's teens are participating. However, if teen customers want to practice DDR in the library, they may be willing to lend their own equipment for use at the library, providing a suitable space is available. The author would further suggest that librarians purchase an up-to-date PDA/cell phone combination such as a Blackberry™ and learn how to use such functions as taking pictures to upload to a computer and sending and receiving text messages. If these items are cost prohibitive, simply asking teens to demonstrate this type of technology is a great way to start communicating with teens one on one and letting them know that librarians are interested in their culture.

In addition to staying abreast of the "hot" technologies that teens like and use, librarians also need to know about teens' reading and viewing interests. One easy way to do this is to place a book/DVD title suggestion box in the teen area. Another great way for librarians to solicit reading requests from teens and learn about what's hot in teen literature is to purchase and install *Reader's Advisor Online,* Libraries Unlimited's readers' advisory database, or *NoveList K-12,* another readers' advisory database, on all of the library's OPACs (online public access computers, aka the electronic card catalog). Both *Reader's Advisor Online* and *NoveList* take the approach of "if you liked Harry Potter, try this" to help teens find books they will enjoy. More information on *Reader's Advisor* and *NoveList* can be found in chapter 4.

The next important consideration is deciding what steps to take if your library does not own the books that teens are requesting. If the library allows teens to suggest titles to purchase or to use *NoveList* to find books to read, then it is imperative to actually obtain the books or DVDs requested, either by purchasing them or by borrowing them from another library. Otherwise, like the user-surly technology responses mentioned previously, when teens realize they will not be able to get these titles, they will quickly lose interest and will not return to the library. In addition to using a suggestion box and *NoveList,* the librarian should also stay abreast of teen reading interests by reviewing such teen book lists as those published by the American Library Association's (ALA's) Young Adult Library Services Association (YALSA). Lists such as Top Picks for Teens, Best Books for Young Adults, and others can be found on the ALA's Web site: www.ala.org.

Finally, librarians who serve teens can continue to learn about these important customers and their interests by doing the following:

- Taking a genuine interest in teens by asking them about their interests.
- Developing a teen library advisory board.
- Staying knowledgeable about local middle and high school sports.
- Viewing movies and TV shows that teens like or visiting www.televisionwith outpity.com for recaps of popular shows.
- Previewing sites like *MySpace* or other social-networking Web sites.
- Checking out teen trends and marketing by skimming teen magazines such as *Teen People* or searching for and scanning popular teen Web sites.
- Skimming music magazines such as *Rolling Stone* and gaming magazines such as *GamePro.*
- Being active in the community and attending school events in which teens are participating.

Knowing what's hot is indeed important, but equally important is knowing what's NOT hot! Some "not hot" items when dealing with teens are listed below:

- Dissing (putting down) technology that teens use.
- Creating rigid library rules and enforcing them rather than asking for input from teens about how their library space should be used and the services they need.
- Being defensive with teens and taking things personally.
- Stereotyping teens rather than getting to know individuals.
- Trying to be a young adult's best friend.
- Being hung up on procedures, rules, and regulations that really are not important.
- Treating teens like adults.
- Treating teens like kids.
- Only selecting literature that you feel is "appropriate" for teens.
- Making the teen space in the library yours rather than theirs.

HOW TO RELATE TO TEENS

It has previously been recommended that library staff should probably not try to emulate young adult customers by using the language that they use, as this will come across as stilted and will not help staff to establish a healthy, professional relationship. However, library staff can certainly ask for clarification when a young adult lapses into slang, and the reverse is also true. Library staff should keep library jargon to a minimum and be ready to explain library terminology in "plain English" to teens rather than using technical terminology as a barrier to keep the young adult customer in his place, so to speak. Conversely, being overly nice by showing a fake smile or referring to teens as "honey," "sweetie," or some other term of endearment is just as dangerous as being cold and unfeeling. The proper approach and tone to use when working with teens is exactly the same as the approach and tone library staff would use with adult customers. Talk to teens in a way that is friendly but professional, respectful, nonjudgmental, and interested. Above all, library staff must be genuine, as teens are definitely savvy and will spot insincerity immediately.

Respect is a Two-Way Proposition

Respect from teens, just as from anyone else, must be earned. One sure way to earn that respect is for library staff to respect their young adult customers. Staff can show respect by taking requests for assistance seriously and giving 100 percent effort whenever providing any type of service to teens. More information about demonstrating respect for young adult customers is included in chapter 2.

Library Rules

For the library to run efficiently and effectively, it is necessary to have rules and regulations as well as policies and procedures. As indicated previously, it is "not hot" for librarians to set rigid rules for the young adult library, but, of course, some rules must be in place for the library to work well. One powerful tool for earning respect from teens is to involve them in developing the rules and regulations and policies and procedures that will govern the teen library. Of course, library staff must also guide teens as they develop the rules so that they are neither overly strict nor overly permissive. Then, after rules are developed, librarians can ask the teens who were involved in formulating them to support and even promote the rules to their peers. This method works much better than the library staff having to call teens' attention to the rules. Some rules about rules are as follows:

- Rather than calling them "rules" for library behavior, consider calling them something less authoritative such as "library expectations," "operating norms," or the like.

- Keep the number of rules to a minimum! No one can be expected to learn and memorize a long laundry list of rules, so try to keep them clear and succinct.
- If possible, post the rules so that teen customers will be able to see them, rather than assuming that your teen customers already know how to behave in the library.
- State the rules positively rather than posting a list of "don'ts." For example: "Be respectful of others' needs for quiet" is much better than "Do not disturb others!"
- The young adult area should not be the only space in the library governed by rules or expectations, so if rules are posted there, you should also post the appropriate rules in the adult area and the children's area.
- Know in advance how library staff will handle those who break the rules, that is, have a set of "rules" (procedures really) that govern the process for dealing with those who break the rules.
- Never, ever post the rules for the teen library on the library's website! This automatically conveys the impression that the library is not teen friendly.
- If staff members are expected to treat teens respectfully and fairly, they should have an equitable set of "consequences" that can be realistically enforced.
- Practice the Three Fs—be friendly, fair, and (when necessary) firm.

Dealing with Behavior Problems

It is inevitable that at some time library staff will have to deal with teens who are breaking rules and causing problems for staff or other customers. If staff members prepare for this situation in advance, chances are they will do a much better job of handling the situation. The following are some suggestions for addressing and dealing with teen behavior problems. First, whenever possible, convey rules and expectations to teens *before* problems arise. New teen customers could be given a tour of the library and an orientation session by a staff member, or even better, by a member of the library's teen advisory board. Create an atmosphere that sets high expectations for behavior, and most of your teen customers will live up to these expectations. If possible, involve teens in developing the rules for using their space and materials in the library. When you discuss the library's rules with teens, talk about the reasons for needing the rules and the negative impact of violating rules, rather than emphasizing "library policies."

When approaching young adults who are behaving improperly, be direct and remind them about the rules. Then ask that they adhere to the rules, and thank them in advance for their cooperation. This indicates to the customers that you believe they will comply with your expectations. Sometimes using nonverbal cues can be as effective as verbally telling teens that they are not behaving appropriately. Such cues as a serious stare, moving closer to the teen, shaking your head, or lowering your own voice can convey your expectations. Of course, the stereotypical "shhhh" is NOT an effective tool, as most teens loathe this type of discipline. Try to intervene in a low-key manner when first approaching teens. If you escalate the situation by raising your voice or being excessively stern, teenagers will respond in kind by being excessively defensive or even aggressive. As much as possible, use "I" statements rather than "you" statements. "I would appreciate you keeping it down please," instead of "You need to stop talking so loudly."

Do NOT wait to enforce rules until you are angry! When teens break the rules, deal with the behavior in a way that is fair and objective rather than losing your temper and your professional demeanor. It is good to have a "severe clause" in your consequences, in which you describe behavior that absolutely will not be tolerated and will result in the perpetrator being asked to leave the library immediately. Behaviors that would fit into this category are those that are illegal, disrespectful, or dangerous to self or others. NEVER use put-downs or personal attacks. Remember, it's about the behavior that is being exhibited. It is NOT about the person. Always be firm and consistent but fair in enforcing rules. Teens are quick to spot unfairness, so despite the fact that library staff members may like some teens better than others, it is imperative to hold all teen customers to the same set of behavioral expectations. Finally, and most important, always model good behavior—the same type of behavior you expect from your teen customers. Just as they can readily see inequities in enforcing the rules, teens are also aware of hypocrisy. Walking the walk is just as important as talking the talk, and this one behavior will go a long way in helping library staff establish positive relationships with teen customers.

Despite the challenges of working with teens in the library, the rewards can be numerous. If young adults have a positive experience in the library, just as they can be zealots about those things that are "hot" in the teen world, they can also become strong advocates for the public library. Teens do indeed have strong friendships and powerful peer networks, and they will definitely tell their friends what they think and how they feel about the public library and its staff. Library staff members need to recognize and respect the fact that teens need their independence yet want generous opportunities for socially interacting with peers. They seek strong personal identities, long for acceptance and a sense of achievement, desire to be recognized by both peers and adults, want clear rules, and appreciate respect from the adults with whom they interact. If these elements are in place, the public library can truly become the teen customer's favorite place to be, and when this happens, other teens will begin to visit the library.

WHEN IN DOUBT, ASK!

Just like adults, teenagers like to offer their opinions and express their feelings about topics of importance to them. If, after reading about teens and their world and actually working with some of them in the library, you still feel that you do not really understand the needs and desires of this group of customers, you can solicit information from the teens themselves via a survey, online questionnaire, or personal interviews.

Even if the library staff has an excellent grasp of teen issues and is proficient in working with teens, administering a survey or questionnaire from time to time will help staff stay current and be more effective in meeting teens' needs for library materials and services.

Many examples of surveys exist, and some Web-based software (such as Survey Monkey) for creating electronic surveys is available. The best method for conducting a teen library survey is to provide an electronic survey that can be accessed via the library's Web site and submitted electronically. If this is not possible, a pencil and paper survey is better than none at all. To make your survey more comprehensive, you may want to include both closed-ended and open-ended questions. However, be careful not to create a survey that is very time consuming to answer, as teens will not want to spend more than about 10 minutes completing it. It is also critical that teen surveys be submitted anonymously. Otherwise, teens will be reluctant even to fill out a survey, much less submit it. Also, prior to conducting such a survey, library staff will need to publicize the survey and explain its purpose. Publicity can be provided via the library Web site, in the local newspaper, in the school library, or by classroom teachers, with permission from the school administration.

Below are some sample questions that can be used. The questions below are open ended in that they cannot generally be answered by a simple "yes" or "no." The questions can be used as they are, or they can be modified to obtain the specific information needed by library staff. The questions progress from general to specific, with the first few questions addressing the teen's world, and the last questions addressing issues specific to the library:

- Tell us about your world. What are the things that matter most to you?
- What is your opinion of technology?
- What are your favorite types of technologies?
- How do you feel about your friends and friendship in general?
- Do you belong to any formal or informal groups? If so, what groups?
- What are the most important issues you deal with?
- What do you consider the "must haves" for today's teens?
- What things, language, and ideas do you think are "lame"?
- What do you like about the public library?
- What do you dislike about the public library?
- What is your general opinion of the public library?
- What are your hobbies or favorite leisure time activities?
- What do you use the public library for?
- How often do you go to the public library?
- What would make you go to the library more often?
- If you were in charge of the public library, what would it be like?
- If you were designing a teen library, what would it look like?
- Do you need help from staff when you go to the library?
- If so, how do you go about getting help?

- Do you usually get what you need when you use the public library?
- Would you be interested in serving on the library's teen advisory board?
- Is so, what do you think this board should do to help the library?
- Anything else you'd like to add?

For those library staff members who have established positive relationships with teen library customers, a personal interview can be another tool to use to solicit input. The advantage to an interview is that the teen will not have to do the writing, which can sometimes be a deterrent to teens who either are not good at writing or do not like to write. Like the written survey, interviews should be brief—a maximum of 10 minutes long. Also, it is important to interview only one teen at a time. Otherwise, peer pressure may influence a teen not to answer questions in the way that she would answer them without the presence of another teen. Be sure to conduct interviews in an area that is relatively quiet but not totally isolated from the rest of the library. Otherwise, the teen may feel uncomfortable being secluded with an adult staff member.

Whether input is solicited from a survey or questionnaire or personal interview, it is critical that parents know about and give their permission for library staff to solicit information from their children. Written permission via a signed form is best. Permission forms should be filed and kept in case they are needed in the future. It is also important to give the parents a copy of the permission form for their records.

Now that you have learned what makes teens "tick," so to speak, it is time to put that knowledge into practice and learn how the library can serve the needs of your teen customers. One of the most important functions that the pubic library provides to teens is reference service, both for homework assignments and for personal needs. Chapter 2 will describe how you can facilitate this valuable service in ways that are effective when working with your teen customers. Questioning styles, resources, and specific interview techniques will be presented; all of these can be implemented without a great deal of formal knowledge or experience. Meanwhile, Web sites to help you continue to learn about the world of today's teens are given below.

WEB RESOURCES

MySpace: http://www.myspace.com—an online social-networking site for teens and adults; teens should be cautioned about Internet safety before using this site.

NetLingo: http://www.netlingo.com—an Internet dictionary that includes technology terms related to Internet use, Internet acronyms for parents, such as "PIR" (parent in room), that teens use in their e-mail messages and chat rooms, and a glossary for those who are new to the Internet.

Pink Is the New Blog: http://www.pinkisthenewblog.com/—a site that includes gossip about celebrities of interest to teens as well as adults

Second Life: http://www.secondlife.com/—an interactive, 3D, digital gaming world in which the site is created by users.

The Shifted Librarian: http://www.theshiftedlibrarian.com/—a blog for progressive librarians who work with teens and want to stay abreast of technology trends.

Spank Mag: http://spankmag.com/—a worldwide online community for youth, teens, and young adults aged 14 to 24; it provides a forum for users, articles of interest, and social-networking functions.

Tametheweb.com: http://www.tametheweb.com—a weblog about libraries and technology developed and moderated by Michael Stephens.

Television without Pity: http://www.televisionwithoutpity.com—a site that includes recaps and reviews of many network programs, as well as a user forum, a free listserv, and other features dealing with television programs.

Y! Music: http://music.yahoo.com/—a site that features videos of performing artists, downloadable music, articles about musicians, and other information of interest to teens who love popular music.

Ypulse: http://www.ypulse.com/—a youth marketing site that presents trends and products of interest to 'tweens and teens in the areas of sports, music, fashion, and culture.

CHAPTER 2

Reality Reference: Assume Nothing

As is the case with adult library customers, providing quality reference services for teens requires excellent communication skills, patience, and perseverance. In fact, providing reference services to teen customers may actually require library staff to possess better communication skills, patience, and perseverance than they use with adult customers, due to the fact that teens may not be as articulate about expressing what they need or may not have a thorough understanding of homework assignments if teachers have not given them all of the necessary information. Most library users are not able to communicate their information needs clearly in the initial phase of searching for information, and teens are no exception.

Today's teens need information about a wide variety of topics to use for school and for personal interests, and it takes skilled, approachable library staff to help them find the information they want and need. This may mean abandoning assumptions or preconceptions and starting with a "blank slate" when a library staff member starts the initial reference interview process with a teen customer. As was discussed previously, teens' communication styles and use of language are not always the same as those of adults, so it is important for library staff to keep an open mind, listen well and deeply, learn good questioning techniques, and be prepared to spend the time necessary to help teen customers obtain the resources and information they need to complete their assignments or satisfy their quest for personal information.

HOW APPROACHABLE ARE YOU?

The initial contact between staff and customers is crucial to the ultimate success or failure of the reference transaction. The Reference and User Services Association (RUSA), a division of the American Library Association, explains in its *Guidelines for Behavioral Performance of Reference and Information Service Providers* that this initial contact and its related behaviors "will set the tone for the entire communication process, and will influence the depth and level of interaction between the staff and the patrons" (Management of Reference Committee, RUSA 2004, 15). If teens do not perceive library staff as approachable, it is unlikely that they will ask for help when it is needed, or accept it when it is offered. Sometimes just making eye contact in a direct but nonthreatening manner, smiling sincerely, and demonstrating a relaxed posture when teen customers approach the reference area will start the reference interview off in a way that fosters success and ensures that the teen customer will return to the library for help in the future. Conversely, not making eye contact with a teen customer, frowning or smiling effusively, or displaying a stiff body posture may be enough to alienate teens immediately, to the extent that they never darken the library door again! Thus, being approachable is indeed a critical element in providing effective reference services to teens.

To establish approachability, the following tips are offered by RUSA:

- Locate reference services in visible areas.
- Use signage to direct customers.
- Be ready to serve customers and give them your undivided attention.
- Acknowledge anyone who is waiting.
- Make eye contact.
- Smile.
- Use friendly body language—stand up, move forward or closer.
- Greet customers.

In addition, RUSA recommends roaming the library when possible, approaching customers to offer assistance, and checking back with them to make sure they are getting what they need (Management of Reference Committee, RUSA 2004, 15). Having to approach someone sitting behind a desk is intimidating even for adults. For teens, desks are closely associated with the classroom and a teacher who has a great deal of power and authority. This mental or emotional association can be a powerful deterrent to teen library customers, to the extent that they immediately decide to leave the reference area and try to find resources on their own. Obviously, this situation does not result in a positive experience for teens, nor, more than likely, will they get what they need from the library's resources. Thus, removing this physical barrier can send a positive message to teen patrons, one that says the staff is approachable and welcoming rather than stern and judgmental. If the library staff member in the reference area does have to sit behind a desk to perform various tasks at the computer or to do paperwork, then when a teen approaches the desk, she or he should immediately stand up and come around to the front of the desk to meet and greet the teen.

Some other strategies to establish approachability include listening without interrupting or jumping to conclusions, encouraging teen customers to take their time in asking questions or explaining assignments, working *with* teen customers rather than *for* them, asking questions rather than giving instructions, giving teen customers adequate time to respond before asking additional questions, and avoiding prejudgment of the customers or their information needs.

Prejudging a teen's information needs is never a good idea, but prejudging a teen's appearance is even worse. Judging teens by their appearance, as was mentioned in chapter 1, is a big mistake. Today's teens are greatly impacted by their peer groups, and librarians must realize that some teens will dress in a manner designed to shock others or to help them fit in with a particular peer group in order to be accepted by their friends. Thus, it is important to respond to the question being asked rather than to the appearance of the teen customer. It is also wise to remember that not all teens wish to be approached, and, in fact, a teen customer may actually view a member of the library staff as being intrusive if she walks up to a teen or follows a teen into the book stacks to offer help. A better choice would be for the library staff member to look up, acknowledge the teen with an encouraging smile, and then wait for the teen to approach the staff member. Another approach would be for the staff member to calmly approach the teen and let him know that she is available to help if he needs assistance, and then return to the desk or other work area and wait for the teen to make an approach. Remember, staff should always respect a teen's need for privacy and space. If the offer for assistance is rejected, it should be taken a clear sign that he or she wishes to be left alone.

GATHERING INFORMATION: A MODEL FOR THE REFERENCE INTERVIEW

Library staff should develop a method of communicating with teen customers to provide the very best in reference service. According to RUSA's *Guidelines for Behavioral Performance of Reference and Information Service Providers,* the heart of this communication is the reference interview. The reference interview can be defined as the questioning process that allows staff to determine the customer's needs. The success or failure of the reference service depends upon clear communication throughout a reference interview that reflects a genuine interest in the customer's needs. Some general rules and guidelines for conducting a successful reference interview are the following.

Assume Nothing

Perhaps the most important part of the reference interaction is the initial point of contact. As was discussed before, it is best not to assume that what is asked for is what is needed. Most library customers, regardless of their age, need help in clarifying their information needs. Do they need information about "euthanasia" or "youth in Asia"? Do they need information about the brain or about medical treatments for migraine headaches? Do they need information about Kung Fu or the Martial arts? Are they seeking information about football teams or the rules of the game of football? Do they need information about stem cell research or about cloning? Is the teen customer looking for information on art or specific painting techniques? Does the teen need information on Native Americans or particular locations of specific tribal groups? Will general information about abortion suffice, or does the teen customer need to know the pros and cons on this issue for a debate in speech class? Library staff should assume nothing and should continue questioning to determine the real information need. Questions should move from broader, more general ones to more specific questions that include finer details, in order to provide the best resources available to answer the questions, whether they are homework related or for personal information.

Distinguish between Homework and Personal Need

While it may be tempting to assume that most reference interactions between library staff and teens are homework or school related, it is best not to make that assumption. However, if possible, it is advisable to make this determination at the very beginning of the interview process so that you can more effectively direct teens to information that is pertinent to what they really need. If the information needed is for homework or is school related, ask to see the requirements of the assignment as written by the teacher or student. Even with the assignment in hand, it may be difficult to interpret what is needed without further questioning. If you are familiar with a specific teacher's typical research assignments, then ask the customer for the name of the teacher who assigned the project. If you are not familiar with the teacher's assignments, take notes as the teen customer describes the requirements of the assignment to you. This will allow you to contact the teacher later, if necessary, to obtain more information so that you can more effectively help the next teen customer who has been given this same assignment.

Of course, the best-case scenario would be to obtain the teachers' assignments in advance so that you can gather needed resources and direct teen customers to them. If you do not have time to contact teachers or access to their contact information, then you may want to find the school's Web site and see if various teachers' research assignments are posted there. This is fairly common practice in today's schools, so you may be able to find most of the major research assignments at the beginning of the school year. If so, it is a good idea to print these assignments and keep them in a file for future use. Also, the teachers' e-mail addresses will be included on the school's Web site as well, so you can contact the teachers with questions about research assignments ahead of time, which will give you a huge advantage when teen customers come to the public library for homework help!

Ask Open-Ended Questions

Asking questions that cannot be answered by a "yes" or "no" response will allow library staff to gain more specific information about what is needed. Some examples include the following:

- Can you tell me more about what you need?
- Is this for a homework assignment or for your personal information?
- Where have you previously looked for information?
- Does your teacher require you to use a specific number and type of resources?
- What do you already know?
- What would you like to know, or what do you need to know?
- What kind of information do you need—simple facts or statistics, in-depth descriptions of various aspects of your topic, comparisons to other topics, historical information, or other information?
- What type of end product does this assignment require, that is, a research paper, bibliography only, speech, PowerPoint presentation, debate, or other product?

Listen Carefully to Responses

Practice good listening skills by allowing plenty of time for responses to questions without interrupting. Maintain eye contact and nod your head when you understand. If you do not understand, continue asking questions in order to solicit more specific information. Take notes if necessary. This will let the teen customer know that you take her or him seriously and want to help. If you have the teacher's assignment, pull the project description and go over it with the young adult to be sure that you are both in agreement on the requirements.

Repeat, Rephrase, and Refine

Make sure you understand what is needed by either repeating or rephrasing the responses. Then ask something like, "Is this what you think you need to complete the assignment?" "If not, what else do you think you need to complete this assignment?" If necessary, keep asking questions until both you and the customer are very clear about what information is needed. One last question might be something like, "Are you completely satisfied with the amount and kind of information you have at this point?"

REFERENCE INTERVIEW EXAMPLES

The following are two reference interview scenarios, including one that is not effective and one that is.

Scenario 1

A teen approaches the reference desk. The library staff member keeps her head down as she is working on a very important, deadline-driven project. Since the teen has not been acknowledged by the staff member, he clears his throat. At this point, with a strained smile on her face, the library staff member curtly asks, "May I help you?"

The teen responds, "Do you have any books about JFK?"

The staff member questions smugly, "Do you mean John Fitzgerald Kennedy, the 35th president of the United States?"

The teen ducks his head and shrugs his shoulder.

The library staff member slowly gets up from behind her desk, straightens the document on which she has been working, and primly places her pen on the desk beside the document. Then she leads the student to the biography section, points out several books about John F. Kennedy, and quickly returns to the reference desk.

A few minutes later, the staff member observes the teen leaving the library empty handed.

Scenario 2

A teen approaches the reference desk. The library staff member looks up, smiles, gets out of her chair, walks to the front of the desk, and the following conversation takes place.

Staff member:	Hello. How can I help you?
Teen:	Do you have any books about JFK?
Staff member:	Yes, we do, but before we take a look, can I ask whether this is a homework assignment?
Teen:	Yeah, but I don't have it with me.
Staff member:	That's OK. We'll discuss the assignment, and I'll ask you some questions to make sure we get exactly what you need to complete the assignment. What specific information about JFK do you need?
Teen:	I don't know, just something about his assassination.
Staff member:	That really helps. So, what do you already know about the assassination?

Teen:	He was killed by some guy, and there's a bunch of theories that it was a conspiracy. I'm supposed to find out more about one of the theories, but I don't know which one.
Staff member:	Let's see if we can figure this out so that I can be sure I understand what you need. Your assignment is to research one of the theories about the Kennedy assassination, but you are not sure which one. Can you give me some details that might help us narrow this down?
Teen:	Well, actually, it has something to do with some video some guy took. I'm working in a group, and I'm supposed to find out about the video.
Staff member:	Let's check the online catalog to find out what books we have on the assassination. We'll pull several of the books that look like they might have some information, and then we can look at the tables of contents and indexes to see whether any of them discuss a video that was made.

Together, the staff member and teen locate a reference book that includes information about the Kennedy assassination and the Zapruder film. The staff member also shows the teen how to access the online catalog and do a keyword search to find additional print material, as well as how to access online periodical databases to get more current information. The teen finds an additional book that gives more background information about the evidence found on the film, as well as a recent article about new methods for examining the film. The library staff member shows the teen how to use the photocopy machine and helps him print the article from the online periodical database.

The difference between the two scenarios is profound. In the first scenario, the teen walks away empty handed and will probably not return to the public library when he needs help with homework assignments. Undoubtedly, the teen perceives the library staff as indifferent, or perhaps even hostile, and the library as useless. In the second scenario, the teen finds several sources of information and perceives the library staff as interested and helpful, and the library as a great place to find pertinent and timely information.

In addition to simply helping teens find specific resources they can use to complete assignments or get personal information, the reference interview is also the perfect time to show teens how to use the library's online catalog, where to find reference books, and how to access online databases or free Web sites for current information. It also gives staff an opportunity to actually take teens to various sections of the library to point out where various types of material in the collection are shelved. Staff can extend the reference service to include a follow-up conversation when the young adult returns to the library. Approaching teens after a successful reference interview and asking if they are finding what they need is a great way of letting teens know that they are valued and that their needs are taken seriously.

A WORD ABOUT VIRTUAL REFERENCE

Not all reference transactions occur within the four walls of the library. It is possible to offer virtual reference services to teens via the library's Web site or e-mail. However, offering this type of service to teens will require a higher level of communication. Today's teens live in a world of immediate communication via the Internet, chat rooms, e-mail, cell phones, and text messaging. If virtual reference services are offered, it is imperative that responses are as immediate as possible, and that all communication is clarified. Teens will not wait several hours or overnight for their questions to be answered, and it is not likely that they will communicate as effectively with library staff online as they would if the transaction were to take place in person. Teens often have their own specialized style of writing when corresponding via electronic means, and the possibilities for miscommunication are much greater in this format. Thus, library staff members who provide virtual reference services need to be mindful of the following:

- The hours that the virtual reference desk is staffed should be convenient for teens.
- Virtual librarians need to be tech savvy.
- Virtual librarians must be able to establish a good rapport via written communication.
- Virtual library staff must be freed from other duties during the times they are providing virtual reference service, so that they can respond in a timely manner.
- It is imperative to have the necessary software in order to make virtual reference services as smooth and easy as possible for customers.
- Virtual reference should never replace in-person services but rather provide options to customers.
- When providing virtual reference services, library staff must include citations so that teen customers will have the documentation needed for research assignments.
- Virtual librarians must at all times be highly professional and objective.
- Virtual librarians should NEVER divulge personal information to teen customers.

Sometimes outside agencies such as state libraries will provide 24/7 virtual reference services free, or for a minimal charge. In Colorado, for example, the *AskColorado* virtual reference service allows users to pose questions 24 hours a day, seven days a week. Questions are sent to volunteer librarians who will answer them within a fairly short period of time. Member libraries throughout the state pay a nominal fee to participate in this service. Pennsylvania also recently implemented a virtual reference service for public and school clientele that is a companion to their Power Library resources. Several commercial vendors provide the same service but typically for a larger fee. It may well be worth paying the cost of these services to better meet the needs of teen customers.

COMMUNICATING WITH TEACHERS AND SCHOOL LIBRARIANS

Teachers and school librarians/media specialists are committed to finding ways to help their students succeed in the classroom and will value communication from the public library staff regarding available services and programs. Likewise, reference staff may gain valuable information about school policies and procedures, upcoming assignments, and other issues that impact their teen customers by frequently communicating with school staff.

The following is a list of suggestions for communicating with local school staff:

- Check district and individual school Web sites for contact information. Note school addresses and phone numbers, as well as contact information for school librarians/media specialists, and teachers.
- Create mail and e-mail lists of contacts for all secondary schools in your area.
- Check for links to school libraries. Look for information about upcoming assignments, subscription databases, citation formats used, subjects taught, and general collection information.
- Also make note of any other links to Web sites that may be useful.
- Relay information to schools about the reference services and products offered at the public library.
- Send schools the library contact information, information about upcoming events and programs, and information about obtaining public library cards.
- Survey teachers and school librarians to determine what services and resources are needed for teachers and teens.
- Ask for ideas for professional resources as well as reference resources for students.
- Ask for assignment alerts for any upcoming projects that might result in a large number of students accessing public library resources.
- Create files for student teachers. Include lesson-planning resources and information about available reference services.
- Provide special library accounts for teachers that give them checkout privileges such as longer circulation periods and unlimited or more generous numbers of items that can be checked out at one time.

DEALING WITH PLAGIARISM

In this age of technology, it has become all too easy for teens to download, copy, and paste the works of others into their own assignments. Sometimes this is intentional, but often it is not. Plagiarism is one of the most serious and most common issues in education today. Although federal copyright law may seem remote to local library users, it is very real and enforceable. Violating copyright law is a serious offense, and teen library users need to be made aware of both the legal and the ethical ramifications of this action. Thus, it is important for library staff to understand and enforce copyright compliance in the library as they are helping teen customers with homework assignments.

The word "plagiarize" means "to steal and pass off [the ideas or words of another] as one's own: use [another's production] without crediting the source" and "to commit literary theft: present as new and original an idea or product derived from an existing source" (*Merriam Webster Online*). Teens must deal with a great deal of information in many formats. For teens, learning how to use that information and incorporate it into their own work is difficult and time consuming. Therefore, it is often very tempting for teens to use another's words as their own, in the hope that no one will notice. Sometimes, in fact, teens have not been taught that this practice is not only unethical but illegal, so they continue to plagiarize until they get caught by a teacher, a librarian, or worse, a legal authority.

Library staff, particularly in the reference area, can provide a very valuable service to their teen customers by sharing with them examples for citing another person's work. If possible, library staff should make available a handout that gives examples of how to paraphrase, quote, and cite sources of information. It is also helpful for library staff to provide citation style sheets for students to use, either in paper format or as links that can be reached from the library's Web site. An excellent online resource is *Plagiarism: What It Is and How to Recognize and Avoid It,* an online pamphlet from Indiana University's Writing Tutorial Services, located at http://www.indiana. edu/~wts/pamphlets/plagiarism.shtml. This site also includes examples of plagiarism and strategies for students to help them avoid plagiarizing.

THE BIG6 AT THE REFERENCE DESK

The Big6 Information Problem Solving Model was created by educators Mike Eisenberg and Bob Berkowitz. It is widely used in schools across the nation and at all grade levels. It is often used as a research model, but it may be used to solve any informational problem or complete any informational task and is an excellent tool to have at the reference desk. The six steps are very easy to follow, and may even provide a means for conducting the reference interview. Posters and bookmarks, as well as many free handouts and fliers, are available on the Big6 Web site. The six steps of the Big6 (Big6 © [1987] Eisenberg and Berkowitz: www.big6.com) are given below:

The Big6™ Skills

1.   Task Definition

   1.1   Define the information problem.
   1.2   Identify the information needed.

2.   Information-Seeking Strategies

   2.1   Determine all possible sources.
   2.2   Select the best sources.

3.   Location and Access

   3.1   Locate sources (intellectually and physically).
   3.2   Find information within sources.

4.   Use of Information

   4.1   Engage (e.g., read, hear, view, touch).
   4.2   Extract relevant information.

5.   Synthesis

   5.1   Organize from multiple sources.
   5.2   Present the information.

6.   Evaluation

   6.1   Judge the product (effectiveness).
   6.2   Judge the process (efficiency).

The Big6 helps provide focus and organization to anyone doing research, performing a task, or solving a problem, and it is an excellent resource for teens who are seeking information and doing research at the library.

TIPS AND TRICKS FOR THE REFERENCE DESK

Several tips and tricks for providing easy access to information and facilitating reference services for library staff and library users, especially teens, at the reference desk, are given below. These ideas and suggestions will provide some quick and easy ways to please teen customers and provide high-quality reference services.

Ask teen customers for their copies of their homework assignments. Make copies as needed, and note teacher names, schools, grade levels, subjects taught, and dates.

Start a file of "assignment alerts" that teachers have submitted for your future use, and include notes about resources found (both print and online) that were helpful, as well as notes for future collection development. File by school, subject, teacher, or grade level—whichever will be most practical for library staff to access. Note: "assignment alerts" are forms that can be distributed by library staff to teachers, to solicit information about upcoming assignments that will require teens to use the library's resources and services. Several samples are available on the Web: simply type "assignment alert" into the search bar of your browser to find them.

Create pamphlets or bookmarks about teen services and programs offered at the library. Include general information about hours and closings, number of items allowed for checkout at one time, overdue policies, interlibrary loan availability, and how to place a hold on library materials.

Create booklists by genre of popular and/or new titles of interest to teens, and have them available either as pamphlets or as bookmarks. Include brief plot summaries and call numbers.

Create lists of useful Web links available for different topics. Place these links on the library's Web site for easy access.

Create lists of popular videos, DVDs, and music CDs available in the library.

Create a handout of citation tools and include information on how to cite sources in both MLA and APA format; include examples of how to paraphrase and quote. Also, include links to online citation tools on the library's Web site.

Have Big6 information available in either handout or bookmark form.

It is also very useful to have the following items available to teens while they are in the library working on projects for school:

- Pens and pencils
- Highlighters
- Colored pencils
- Sticky notes
- Sticky page flags
- Whiteout
- Lined notebook paper
- Lined note cards
- Poster board
- Paper clips
- Stapler
- Hole puncher
- Data discs and blank CDs for saving/transferring computer files
- Portable USB drives, also known as jump drives, flash drives, or thumb drives (Consider having more than one available for checkout as these are rather expensive.)
- Inexpensive calculators
- Computers for word processing, creating spreadsheets, and creating Power-Point slideshows
- CD players and DVD players for listening and viewing.

While it may seem that this list is long and the items on it are perhaps expensive to collect, teen library users will greatly appreciate having them available for use. If the cost of providing these materials is too great, consider asking for donations from the community, or selling the supplies at a minimal cost. This can sometimes be an easy and effective ongoing fund-raiser for the library.

TYPES OF REFERENCE MATERIAL

The following list of reference resources provides a starting place for developing a reference collection that can be used by both teen and adult library customers. See Margaret Irby Nichols' excellent Web document, *Selecting and Using a Core Reference Collection,* listed in the Web Resources section at the end of this chapter, for a thorough guide to developing a sound reference collection for your library.

The Basics

General encyclopedias such as *World Book* or *Encyclopedia Americana* are good resources to use at the beginning of many research projects, because they provide general overviews of various topics. Consider purchasing at least one online encyclopedia, as these are typically updated more frequently and provide useful supplemental material such as information on current events and historical time lines. In addition, the keyword search feature sometimes makes it easier to find information without knowing the specific terms included in a print encyclopedia's index.

Your library should have both abridged and unabridged dictionaries, and, as with encyclopedias, online dictionaries should be available. A thesaurus (available both in print and online) is also a basic reference tool.

Both world atlases and road atlases should be included in the collection. These vary greatly in price and coverage, so shop carefully before purchasing them. In addition, the collection should include a road atlas for your specific state.

The latest edition of the *World Almanac and Book of Facts* is an important reference tool and should be included in the reference collection. Note: if an entire class or grade level in the high school has been assigned a research project on the same topic and information can be found in the *World Almanac,* the library will need to have multiple copies of this work. Inexpensive paperback copies are available, but they will not hold up over a long period of time.

A geographical dictionary or gazetteer is also considered a basic reference tool. As with other reference works, the coverage and price of such an item varies, but inexpensive editions are available.

Specialized Reference Resources

In addition to general encyclopedias, many subject encyclopedias exist. As is logical, these encyclopedias are narrower in scope in that they cover only one or a few topics, but, unlike general encyclopedias, they are more comprehensive in nature. Subject encyclopedias include music encyclopedias, art encyclopedias, science encyclopedias, and numerous others. Since these are specialized, they can be quite expensive, so library staff must evaluate cost versus use when deciding whether to purchase them.

Biographical dictionaries also abound and are quite varied. Some cover only living persons; others only include famous people of the past who are no longer living. While these types of dictionaries do not typically provide comprehensive coverage, they can be good starting places for teens who are doing research on a particular person.

Special dictionaries such as dictionaries of slang, rhyming dictionaries, science dictionaries, music dictionaries, mathematics dictionaries, dictionaries of poetry, and others can also be useful tools when teen customers need to find the definition of a particular word or term that they have encountered when working on a research project in a specific subject area. As is the case with general dictionaries, these materials generally include pronunciation keys and definitions, and they sometimes include other features such as lists of synonyms.

Other specialized reference resources include yearbooks, handbooks, bibliographies, directories, and indexes. Unless your library is a brand new facility in which you are charged with selecting the opening day collection, most of the materials mentioned above will already be included in the reference collection.

Professor, author, and editor Blanche Woolls believes it would be "an interesting experiment for the high school librarian and the public librarian to join forces to buy expensive reference books and have them available in the public library in the summer even if they are on school shelves during the school year" (e-mail to the author). She suggests that the school district and public library could share the cost of these materials and leave them in the public library where they would be accessible in the evening when the school library is closed. This arrangement would help both organizations provide teens with access to more expensive types of reference sets whose wealth of information could be quite beneficial. In addition, this type of partnership and resource sharing is what libraries are all about.

Electronic Reference Resources

In today's public library, online resources and Web-based resources are common. Many of your library's customers will already know how to use these types of reference materials—especially your teen customers—and they will come to the library expecting to find these electronic tools. In fact, almost all of the reference tools mentioned previously come in electronic format as well as in print format. The decision about whether to provide a reference tool in print or in electronic format is based on factors such as cost, availability of computers, staff time for training, and your library's collection policy. Some common electronic reference resources include online periodical databases, research databases for a specific subject area such as science, general research databases that include many other databases for one subscription price, selection tools such as *Books in Print Online,* free Web reference tools such as dictionary. com, and free search engines such as Google. Library staff must decide not only what electronic reference tools to include in the collection but also how these tools will be organized, that is, by means of a one-stop reference approach in which every computer in the library provides access to all electronic resources, organized by topic or some other scheme that is a common configuration, or by means of specific computer reference stations that provide access only to certain types of electronic reference tools such as free Web sites. If the library allows teen customers to use e-mail and chat rooms on computers, for example, maybe not all computers should provide access to every type of activity or function. These decisions should be made well in advance of organizing the reference collection for teen customers.

In summary, giving teens high-quality reference services and resources will demonstrate to these customers not only that the public library does indeed meet vital needs but also that the public library staff members are friendly and genuinely interested in serving them. The reference experience can therefore become a means of establishing a positive rapport with teens that may entice them to return to the library for personal reading materials and perhaps participate in programs that are offered. At the least, a successful reference experience will give teens a more positive attitude toward the public library staff and the services provided; this is definitely a win/win situation!

WEB RESOURCES

The Big6 Information Skills for Student Achievement: http://www.big6.com/—a site including information, suggestions, tips, lesson plans, and many more resources for introducing and implementing the Big6 Information Problem Solving Model.

Digital/Virtual Reference Service: http://www.libraryhq.com/digref.html—an Internet portal with access to articles, electronic discussion lists, bibliographies, forums, discussion lists, and more, all dealing with virtual reference services in libraries.

Guidelines for Behavioral Performance of Reference and Information Service Providers, Management of Reference Committee, Reference Services Section, Reference and User Services Association (a division of the ALA): http://www.ala.org/ala/rusa/rusaprotools/referenceguide/guidelinesbehavioral.htm—a reference guide that provides information about the skills and attitudes necessary for providing quality reference services to library users.

Guidelines for Implementing and Maintaining Virtual Reference Service, Prepared by the MARS Digital Reference Guidelines Ad Hoc Committee, Reference and User Services Association, 2004. Approved by the Reference and User Services Association (RUSA) Board of Directors, June 2004. http://www.ala.org/ala/rusa/rusaprotools/referenceguide/virtrefguidelines.htm—reference guide that includes information about the skills, practices, and attitudes necessary for providing quality virtual reference services to library users.

The Landmark Project's Son of Citation Machine: http://citationmachine.net/—a free online tool for students who need to create citations and bibliographies for research papers and projects.

Reference Materials Collections: http://www.cln.org/subjects/refmat.html—a site including many links to sites that give information on reference materials or provide additional links to such materials.

Selecting and Using a Core Reference Collection, 4th Edition, by Margaret Irby Nichols: http://www.tsl.state.tx.us/ld/pubs/corereference/ internal—a thorough guide to selecting a basic reference collection for libraries.

CHAPTER 3

The Teen Collection

COLLECTION POLICY DEVELOPMENT

Every library needs a written collection policy and procedures that provide guidelines and instructions for staff in three areas: (1) *collection development,* which addresses such items as the kinds of material that will be included in the library's collection, the criteria or standards that material must meet in order to be placed in the collection, the decision as to who is responsible for selecting material, the process for selecting material, the ways to handle gifts and memorial items, and the processes governing the actual purchase and preparation of material to be included in the collection; (2) *collection maintenance,* which includes such items as "weeding" or "deselecting" materials (which simply means removing materials that are out of date, damaged, or no longer needed in the collection), repairing material, organizing material so that it is accessible to the library's customers, reevaluating the collection to make sure that the material is still of value and useful to customers, and replacing worn material; and (3) *challenged material,* which addresses how the library staff will deal with customer complaints about material in the library's collection.

If the library does not have a collection policy, library staff will need to create one. Although this may seem a daunting task, many, many excellent examples are available in the form of printed books or manuals that are available from library publishers, as well as electronic samples available (usually free) on the World Wide Web. The Web Resources section at the end of this chapter lists several sample policies available on the Web. Note that these policies should not be used as they are but should be adapted to meet the needs of the particular community and customers that your library serves. Remember that it is OK to start with bare bones, basic policy and then add to the policy as needed.

Before a policy can be written, library staff will need to gather some pertinent information by assessing the library's community and looking at the demographics of the community, as well as determining the overall purpose of the library's collection and developing the basic philosophy that will guide collection development. Although these tasks may seem quite challenging, they are manageable and do not require a vast knowledge of library science.

Assessing Your Library's Community

First, assessing the community can be done in a simple, informal manner by simply imagining that you are describing your community to someone who has never been there. What is the geographical makeup of the community—mountains, desert, plains, or other terrain? From that question, one can deduce what types of recreational activities are popular, the weather conditions in each season, the vegetation that is prevalent, and other physical characteristics of the community. Since the library's collection typically has informational material on these environmental features, once you identify them, it will be easy to select books and other material that cover the type of environment in your community.

Two other factors to consider in assessing the community are the number of people in the community who have library cards and the number of items that have "circulated," that is, been checked out over a certain time period. Your collection will need to be large enough to accommodate your users' needs, so the library's materials budget will need to be adequate to purchase enough items to meet these needs on a regular basis. It is also helpful to gather such information as the number and types of churches or religious organizations that are in your community, as your collection will need to include information on these and perhaps other religious groups.

Since this book specifically addresses teen library services, it is important to assess your teen community as well. Some aspects to examine are the number of teenagers living in your community, the number of teens who have library cards, the types of recreation in which the teens in your community take part, the hobbies in which your teen customers engage, popular teen social centers in the community, the type of music your community's teens like, local heroes that teens in your community admire, community sports and other competitive activities in which teens participate, and other community facts and issues that impact teens.

It is also important to know about the other information services and resources that are available in your community, such as school libraries, church libraries, and museums, as well as other libraries or library systems in neighboring communities from which materials can be borrowed. Your library's collection, especially the teen collection, should complement rather than duplicate these other resources, so not only is it important to know about these other information resources in the community prior to developing a collection policy, but it is also important to communicate with those charged with developing these other collections, so that all of you can provide the broadest and most complete collections possible to meet the community's needs. The more information you have about your community, the easier it will be to write a collection policy—especially the selection section of the policy, which describes the types of material that will be chosen for the collection.

Demographics

Another important part of the pre-policy assessment includes examining your community's demographics, that is, the statistical information about the economy, ethnic makeup of the community, age ranges and distributions, politics, culture, income levels, educational levels, primary industries or vocations, educational levels, and other factors. Examining demographics may seem overwhelming. However, most towns have a chamber of commerce or visitors' bureau that will have this type of information readily available, so the staff of your library only needs to find this agency and ask for the information rather than having to gather and compile it. Another valuable source for this type of information is your state library. In fact, the state library is an excellent resource for many types of services, so it is a good idea to start there whenever you have questions, need help, or want to find resources on a multitude of library-related topics.

Sections of the Collection Policy

Once you gather the necessary information and are ready to write a policy, you will need to decide what specific sections to include. As stated previously, many different models are available, some with very few sections and pages and some that are quite comprehensive. A basic collection policy includes the following sections.

Introduction: This section clarifies the intent of the policy, for example, providing guidance and direction to the library staff members responsible for collection development and maintenance as well as a very general description of the types of material that will be included in all of the library's collections, including the adult collection, the teen collection, and the children's collection.

Purpose: This section describes the overall purpose of the library's "core collection" (the basic foundation of materials that will be included in the collection) for all library customers, that is, adults, teens, and children. In other words, the purpose section describes what needs the core collections will meet, for example, providing works of literary merit; works that have historical value, informational value, recreational value, educational value, and so on. To take one example, the Spokane, Washington, public library's collection development policy indicates that the young adult collection will serve customers aged 12 to 18 and will primarily include materials for recreational reading, such as popular fiction, graphic novels, bound comic books, magazines, and audio books. The policy further states that all nonfiction materials for teens will be shelved in the adult collection in the branch libraries (Spokane Public Libraries 2003, 13; also see the Web Resources section at the end of the present chapter).

Philosophy: This is the "big picture" section of the document, which describes the ongoing approach to collection development that the librarians will follow. The philosophy statement that undergirds your collection policy answers such questions as whether the collection will be well rounded and complete or composed of a limited number of materials of only the highest quality, whether a wide range of topics will be included in the collection or a narrower approach will be used, and whether the primary intent is to educate and inform or to enrich the lives of customers.

Typically, most public libraries have very broad collections that meet a wide range of needs, rather than a narrow range of materials that meet the needs of only a small segment of the community. Thus, the library's philosophy of collection development might be to have something for everyone in the community who will be using the facility. However, since teens tend to want to read and use the same materials that their peers are using, the philosophy and approach to collection development for the teen collection may be different from that for the adult or children's collection. Public librarians usually remain responsive to customer requests for materials, so that the collection will continue to be viable and meet the needs of the community. Because teen customers can sometimes be more particular about what they will read and use, the collection development philosophy for your library may be to encourage teens to be more involved in guiding the selection of materials for their collection than adult customers in guiding the selection of materials for theirs.

Finally, the philosophy section of the policy should include some guiding documents that describe the overall philosophy and functions of all libraries. These guiding statements have been prepared and adopted by the ALA, and they include such documents as the Library Bill of Rights, the Freedom to Read and Freedom to View statements, and others, available on the ALA Web site at http://www.ala.org.

Collection development: This section describes how library staff will continue to grow and develop the collection to meet the ongoing needs of the customers. The major part of the collection development section deals with selection of materials and describes the "who, what, how, when, and how much" of selecting materials for the collection. It specifies the staff person or persons who will be responsible for selecting materials for the library, the types of materials that will be selected, the process for selecting and acquiring (purchasing) materials, the timing for selecting and purchasing materials, and general guidelines for the library materials budget. The selection portion of the policy also addresses such items as how gifts of money or materials will be handled and the specific criteria that will be used for selecting all types of materials.

Collection maintenance: This section of the policy addresses the question of how the current collection will be maintained and preserved. It includes such areas as repairing damaged materials, preserving material of a historical nature, removing from the collection items that no longer have value, and replacing items that are still needed but have become worn or damaged. For the teen collection, library staff may decide to do a minimum amount of repair and instead focus on replacement of those items that are still popular but have become old, worn, or damaged. Teens are highly selective in the types of material they will check out and are also typically more progressive in the types of technology and equipment they will use. Keeping pace with teens' needs and reading preferences is a challenging but rewarding part of providing library services to this group. Thus, library staff may need to examine and reevaluate the teen collection frequently to determine what needs to be repaired or replaced.

Challenged material: From time to time, a library customer may issue a complaint about an item in the library's collection and may even seek to have the item removed from the collection. Many times, complaints come from parents who wish to protect their young children or teenage children and do not want them exposed to ideas and information that conflict with their family's values. Since many books written for today's teens contain issues and ideas that could be considered graphic or controversial, it is critical that the library's collection policy should include a section on dealing with these complaints. The policy should also provide a formal process for reevaluating material that customers have asked staff to remove from the collection.

SELECTION FOR TEENS

Selection means exactly what the word implies, choosing material to purchase for the library's collection. Careful selection is always important, but for the teen collection it is absolutely critical! Teens want the "latest and greatest" titles in books they read, as well as in audiovisual and computer-based programs. This does not mean, of course, that classic literature should not be included in the teen collection, but it does mean that the classics should be attractive and in a format that is appealing. For example, if the library still has its original copy of *Tom Sawyer* with a cover illustration that is faded and dated looking, or even worse, no cover art at all, then it should probably be replaced by a newer edition with appealing cover art. Both popularity and practicality are important considerations when library staff members are making selections for teens. If items selected for the teen collection do not have popular appeal or relevance for teens, they will be "shelf sitters" that will soon collect dust!

Selection Criteria

The selection criteria are the heart of the library's collection policy, as they provide clear guidelines to library staff about what to purchase and also how to evaluate gifts and donations to the library to make sure that they fit within the overall collection policy. Thus, it is important to formulate criteria that will result in library staff continuing to develop an up-to-date, high-quality collection for customers, especially teen customers. As with the other sections of the collection policy, many examples are available, so it is not necessary for staff to write criteria from scratch. Some general considerations are given below. Note that this is not an exhaustive list but simply some of the criteria that should be considered. Each individual library's staff should examine these criteria in light of the purpose and philosophy of the library's policy, specifically the part of the policy that addresses the teen collection. In general, materials selected should meet the following criteria:

- They should be valid, accurate, and timely.
- They should be of high quality in content, format, and presentation, that is, logically organized, well bound, and attractive.
- They should be accurate, credible, and authoritative.
- They should be appealing to customers.
- They should be balanced and represent varied viewpoints on controversial topics.
- They should be nonbiased (in the case of nonfiction and reference material).
- And they should be priced reasonably, considering the format and content.

Selection Tools

"Selection tools" is library jargon for resources that will help you decide what to purchase. Many excellent selection tools are available, some free or inexpensive and some quite expensive. However, one important point to note is that publishers' catalogs are NOT selection tools but rather advertisements, so be aware that if you use these to select books or other items, what you get may not be what you wanted. As they should, publishers are trying to sell their books, so their catalog "blurbs" are written to make every book sound like a must-have item! Thus, library staff should instead use reputable selection tools that include reviews of material that are written by professional librarians, teachers, or experts in a field. A few examples of selection tools that can be used to select material for teens are given below:

Magazines

- *Voice of Youth Advocates (VOYA)*—published by the ALA
- *Booklist*—published by the ALA
- *School Library Journal*—published by Reed Business Systems

Books

- *Teen Genreflecting: A Guide to Reading Interests*—by Diana Tixier Herald, published by Libraries Unlimited

- *High/Low Handbook: Best Books and Web Sites for Reluctant Teen Readers*—by Ellen V. Libretto and Catherine Barr, published by Libraries Unlimited
- *A Core Collection for Young Adults*—by Patrick Jones, Patricia Taylor, and Kirsten Edwards, published by Neal Schuman Publishers, Inc.
- *H. W. Wilson's High School Catalog*—published by H. W. Wilson Company

Web Sites

- American Library Association—www.ala.org (This site includes several lists of books, such as best books for teens and award-winning books for teens.)
- Follett Library Resources' Titlewave—www.flr.titlewave.com (Although this is a book vendor's site, many reviews included on the site were originally published in professional selection publications such as *Booklist* and *School Library Journal*.)
- Permabound's Web site—www.permabound.com (See comments on Follett's Titlewave.)
- Baker and Taylor's Web site—www.btol.com (See comments on Follett's Titlewave.)

Subscription Databases

- *NoveList K-12*
- *Books in Print with Reviews*—produced by Bowker
- *Libraries Unlimited's Web site*—produced by Libraries Unlimited

COLLECTION MAINTENANCE

In addition to selecting new materials for the library's collection, library staff must also decide whether to keep or weed (remove) items that are no longer useful, are out of date, are damaged, have been replaced by a newer edition, or are unattractive due to damage or age. In addition to weeding these types of materials, library staff must also decide how to preserve and repair materials from time to time. Such factors as the library budget, staff time, and staff expertise will impact decisions about collection maintenance, as will the library's collection development policy. Your library may decide that it is not worth the staff's time and energy to try to repair damaged material; instead, when materials are damaged, they will simply be replaced. On the other hand, if the budget is very limited, as is often the case in small libraries, it may be necessary for library staff to learn how to repair books and other materials. The decision to weed or repair materials must be considered in light of these factors, and standards and procedures should be included in the collection policy.

Weeding the Library's Collection

Weeding or deselection is just as important as the selection of new material for the collection. Many detailed guides and methods for weeding are available, some of which are included in the Web Resources section at the end of this chapter, but some general suggestions are given here:

- Weeding should be done by section, on a rotating basis rather than weeding the entire collection at one time.
- Library staff should develop and use a weeding schedule, and weeding should be ongoing.
- Weed more time-sensitive sections of the collection more frequently. Areas of the nonfiction collection such as those dealing with technology and social sciences, for example, need to be weeded more often than fiction, literature, art, or poetry.
- As new formats replace older ones (for example, as CDs replace cassette tapes), and the budget permits, material in older formats should be weeded and replaced in current formats. Not only will the older type of material cease to be available at some point, but the equipment needed to use the material will become obsolete.
- Weed items that are no longer viable for the collection, such as those that have been found to contain inaccurate information, those that are old and musty smelling, and those that have been replaced by newer editions; older editions that are no longer accurate or complete; items that no longer have significance to your collection, such as fiction that is no longer popular or read; and items that are severely damaged.
- Keep award-winning and classic literature, but when specific items become worn or dated looking, replace them with newer editions.
- Remember: weeding is a journey, NOT a destination, so it is an ongoing process.

Repairing Items in the Collection

Staff must also decide whether to repair items that have minor damage and how to repair heavily damaged or aged materials, such as local history resources, that may have permanent value to the collection. If the library staff decides to repair damaged items, then supplies and equipment designed for this purpose should be purchased from a reputable library vendor. Also, unless staff members are very talented in making and repairing things, they should NOT attempt to repair books and other items. Unattractively mended books will sit on the shelf, and the staff time needed to make repairs could be spent in more effective ways, such as working with teen customers to help them with homework assignments or giving a mini book talk on the newest young adult fiction books.

Your library's collection policy should address all of the aspects of collection maintenance and provide guidelines for weeding and repair of materials, particularly for the teen collection. Since teenagers have very high standards for the types of materials that they will check out and use, it is imperative for the teen collection to look appealing and remain current and relevant to teens' needs. One need only watch and compare the tastes and habits of adult customers versus teen customers to realize that while adults will sometimes use materials that are old and worn looking, teens will usually use only materials that are attractive and up to date. Remember, once a book is a shelf sitter, it will remain a shelf sitter. Although it may seem extravagant to purchase new materials for the teen collection rather than to repair items with minor damage, if the collection is not being used, it is taking up valuable shelf space, and you may be losing teen customers who are future taxpayers and who, therefore, are your potential future funding sources.

Challenged Materials

When parents or other adult customers issue a verbal complaint about material in the teen collection, it is critical that library staff respond in a manner that is neutral and objective. To become emotional or try to defend a particular book or other item may further antagonize the person issuing the complaint. Further, debating the merits of a book with an angry parent will only result in a verbal sparring match that can have no positive outcome. Then what should library staff do when a complaint is issued? The answer is first to be respectful and polite, and listen to the complaint. Then, staff should follow the library's board-adopted procedures for dealing with complaints about material. The collection policy should include a clear process for dealing with complaints, and library staff should be familiar with this process. Note: if an item meets the selection criteria and is within the scope of the type of information or pleasure reading material that the library provides, then it is a legitimate selection and should be retained. However, immediately taking this stance may exacerbate the situation, so it is best to hold information about policies and selection criteria until a later time, when the customer has had an opportunity to further think about the complaint.

If, after listening to the customer and providing him with brief information about the library collection, the library staff member finds that the customer is still not satisfied with the response to the complaint, then, if there is a supervisor on staff, the customer should be referred to the supervisor. However, it is important for the supervisor to know the situation BEFORE being confronted by an angry customer. Thus, rather than simply handing the situation off to the supervisor, the library staff member should write down the customer's name and contact information and let the customer know that the supervisor will contact him. If there is no supervisor on staff and the library staff member has (1) examined the item to make sure that it does indeed meet the selection criteria, (2) provided the customer with basic information about the library's collection, and (3) determined that the customer is not going to withdraw the complaint, then the staff member should provide a "Request for Reconsideration" form so that the customer can file a formal challenge.

It is best to wait for a period of time before giving the customer the Request for Reconsideration form because often, after a customer has had time to rethink the situation, he will decide not to pursue the complaint. Thus, the library staff member can tell the customer that she would like to gather some additional information and forms and then meet the customer again to discuss the next steps to be taken. The staff member can at that point either take the customer's contact information and let the customer know that she will contact him within the next week or set an appointment with the customer to meet him again for a specific date in the near future.

As mentioned earlier, often parents make complaints about controversial material in the library's collection in an effort to "protect" their children from ideas or information they consider to be harmful or threatening to their family's values. This is entirely appropriate. In fact, library staff should be pleased that parents are involved in their children's lives and are interested in what their children are reading, viewing, listening to, or exposed to on the Internet. What is NOT appropriate is for a parent to decide that no one else's child should be able to use the material and that it should be removed from the collection. This is the point at which the parent becomes a censor who seeks to judge the library's collection as well as to limit other customers' access to the material. While library staff should affirm a parent's rights and responsibilities as a parent, they should not allow any parent to determine what is appropriate for all other teens; nor should a library staff member impose her or his own moral, ethical, or religious views or be guided by personal opinion when selecting or deciding whether to retain an item for the collection.

The ALA provides many foundational philosophical documents, such as the Library Bill of Rights and the Freedom to Read statement, that describe basic principles for the library profession. Library staff should read these documents and also include them in the library's collection policy. When in doubt about whether you are selecting materials or censoring materials, ask whether you are attempting to be inclusive as you select items, or exclusive. The difference between these two attitudes is critical!

If your library already has a collection policy in place, congratulations! You are very fortunate that someone else has already done this work. However, your collection policy will still need to be reexamined from time to time to ensure that it is still accurate and usable. Also, keep in mind that typically the entire collection development policy is approved by the governing board of a library, so if a policy needs to be written, it is important that library staff work with the board throughout the process and get board approval before implementing the policy.

TYPES OF MATERIAL AND ACCESS

Types of Material

The library's collection includes many different formats, from books to streaming video, some of which are physically located within the four walls of the library and some of which can be accessed from remote locations such as home or school. Basically, material falls into three categories: print, media, and electronic. Print material includes such items as books, magazines and newspapers, brochures, fliers, primary source documents, and other tangible material in paper format. Media includes such items as music CDs, CD ROMs of books, videotapes and DVDs, and books on tape. Electronic collections include such items as e-books, databases, streaming video, Web resources, downloadable audio, and virtual collections of resources that may include some of the previously mentioned items. It is important that the library's teen customers know what types of material are available, where the material is located, and how to access it. In other words, the library must provide both physical and intellectual access to the collection in ways that are customer friendly and time efficient.

Print Material

Books

The teen collection should include a variety of both fiction and nonfiction books, covering a wide range of reading and interest levels. An excellent resource for selecting fiction for teens is *Teen Genreflecting: A Guide to Reading Interests,* by Diana Tixier Herald (2003). Complete information on this work can be found in the bibliography at the end of this book. The library's teen fiction collection will include not only a variety of genres of popular teen novels, as described in chapter 4, but also adult novels that are appropriate for teens. Recommended lists of these types of adult novels can be found on the Young Adult Library Service Association's (YALSA's) Web site at http://www.ala.org/ala/yalsa/yalsa.htm, as well as on numerous other state and professional organizations' reading lists and Web sites. Just as with fiction, teens will use nonfiction books written specifically for their age group, as well as nonfiction books written for adults that include topics of interest or information that teens need to complete homework assignments. Thus, when selecting nonfiction books, library staff should include popular topics for adult patrons as well as informational books that align with the curriculum being taught in the community's schools.

As mentioned previously, fiction books in the teen collection will need to cover a wide range of reading levels and interests. Teens with more advanced reading abilities will be attracted to adult fiction books that contain more complex plots, character development, and other literary elements, whereas teens who are struggling or reluctant readers will need books that fall into the category of high/low books. This category includes books that are of high interest to teens but are written on a lower reading level. Although it can be difficult to find high/low books that are both easy to read and appealing to older children, excellent resources are available to help library staff select these materials. One such example is the *High/Low Handbook: Best Books and Web Sites for Reluctant Teen Readers,* by Ellen V. Libretto and Catherine Barr (2002). Complete information on this book is included in the bibliography at the end of this book. Libretto and Barr's book includes a core (basic) collection of titles for struggling readers, a list of adult materials for reluctant readers, Web resources, a list of publishers who specialize in high/low books, and several helpful indexes. More will be said about types and genres of fiction books in chapter 4.

Magazines and Newspapers

Many magazines written specifically for teens are available. These magazines cover items such as fashion advice, dating, school issues, popular celebrities, music and movies, teen culture, popular technologies, and other topics of interest to teens. Magazine "jobbers" such as EBSCO or Cox Periodicals provide catalogs of magazine titles with brief descriptions. In addition, lists of popular teen magazines can be found on the Web sites of many public or school libraries. Library staff can search for "teen magazines" and find many such lists. If your library has a teen advisory board, its members can help select teen magazines. However, library staff will need to examine the list of titles to ensure that they meet the selection criteria included in the library's collection policy.

Although newspapers specific to teens exist, many in the form of electronic newspapers on the Web, the most common types of newspapers that teens will use are the ones that adult customers use. Thus, it may not be necessary to purchase commercial newspapers specifically for teen customers. However, it would be prudent for the library to make available copies of any newspapers that are published by students in the community's schools. These newspapers are sometimes very well written, and they definitely include news and topics of interest to teen customers. Most school newspapers are available free of charge. Library staff should contact the journalism teacher(s), who can explain how to obtain copies of the newspaper. Regarding electronic newspapers for teens, library staff should screen these publications just as print newspapers are screened, to be sure they meet the selection criteria. If so, library staff can either bookmark these sites on computers in the libraries or provide links to the newspapers from the teen section of the library's Web site, if such a section exists.

Graphic Novels

Although graphic novels are indeed books, because this format is quite different from most other books, it will be addressed separately. Graphic novels are similar to comic books in that they contain many colorful pictures (graphics) and less text than typical novels. This format differs from that of comic books in that graphic novels are longer and usually contain a complete story rather than the serial stories included in monthly comic book publications. Because of the sparse text, graphic novels sometimes appeal to reluctant or struggling readers. However, some graphic novels contain complex plots and characters, so not all titles will appeal to this group of teens. Within the graphic novel format are several different types of novels.

Two popular Japanese graphic novel styles are manga and anime. Manga covers a range of genres from romance and science fiction to realistic fiction and mystery. Popular superheroes such as Batman and Spiderman are featured in manga as well. Anime derives from Japanese animated TV shows and movies and features well-known characters from these productions. The characters are drawn in a stylized manner that makes them very distinctive and recognizable. As with other print books, many resources are available to help library staff select a collection of graphic novels that is appealing and will be well used.

One point to note: graphic-style nonfiction books are now being published, so a more accurate label for books in graphic format is simply "graphic books" rather than "graphic novels," or perhaps "graphic nonfiction" to distinguish these books from graphic fiction books. Some of the graphic nonfiction books can be very useful for reluctant or struggling readers, and because this format is so popular, it may be beneficial for library staff to recommend to these teens that they start with graphic nonfiction books when they have a need for factual information for classroom assignments or for their personal interests. However, since the graphic format may not necessarily be accepted by teachers as viable for research assignments, teens may be limited to using this format as a starting point for assignments. Library staff should check with classroom teachers before promoting graphic nonfiction books for research projects.

Nonprint Material

Media

Many forms of media exist today, and the formats seem to continually evolve at a rapid pace! Small libraries with limited budgets may not be able to keep up with these ever-changing formats, so library staff members who purchase media items need to be highly selective as to both format and content. Also, if the library checks out media, teen customers will need access to the equipment on which to "play" the media. Library staff may need to decide whether equipment will be provided on a check out basis or whether it will be assumed that when teen customers check out a media item, they have the equipment necessary to use it.

Shelving media can sometimes be challenging, so library staff will need to consider the shelf space available as well as customer access when making decisions about the location of media material. Such items as music CDs, CD ROMs, videos/DVDs, and recorded books can either be shelved in a separate area for teens or simply included in a general collection that is accessible to both teens and adults. Both the physical layout and the floor space of the library will influence the decision as to which approach is used. While it is desirable to separate teen media and shelve the collection in the teen area, this may not be possible. One approach that can be used is to inter-shelve media with books. In this arrangement, all material is shelved together in the standard alphabetical or Dewey number order. The advantage to this shelving arrangement is that all materials on a specific topic are located in the same place to provide easy access by customers. The disadvantage is that sometimes library shelves do not accommodate irregular sizes of material, so media material can sometimes get lost on the shelves and not be as accessible as if the material were located on special shelving made for DVDs, for example. Library staff will need to think about these issues before deciding where the media collection will be kept.

Electronic Resources

More and more it seems that electronic resources are becoming available, Some of them complement the physical collection. Some may replace items in the physical collection, and some of these can be quite costly while others are free. When making decisions about selecting and purchasing material, library staff will want to research the various electronic materials that are available and consider the customers' needs and the place in the overall collection that electronic resources will best fill. Some specific examples are as follows.

E-Books

These are usually full-text books that can be accessed electronically on computers or by using special reading devices. While teen customers would probably not want to read a novel in this format, they might want to use a searchable e-book to retrieve information needed for a classroom assignment. Some advantages of e-books are that they do not take up valuable shelf space and multiple copies can sometimes be used simultaneously. Some disadvantages are that e-books can sometimes be quite expensive, and they have to be installed on a computer or downloaded to an external device.

Online Databases

Electronic databases are typically purchased on a subscription basis and need to be renewed annually. These databases are accessed via the World Wide Web, so computers will need to have Internet access to support them. Databases can be found to cover virtually every topic imaginable, and they are available in various formats, including encyclopedias; periodical databases with a variety of magazines, newspapers, and other periodically produced publications; topic-specific databases such as those that are limited to science, literature, history and geography, and other subjects; and many others. Vendors of electronic databases are plentiful, and prices vary greatly, depending upon such considerations as the number of computers or users that will access the database and the number of databases being provided by a specific vendor. Library staff can search the Web for "electronic databases" to access a large list of vendors and types of databases.

Streaming Video

If you have ever accessed a Web site or received an e-mail attachment that included a video clip, you have experienced streaming video. While these examples are of isolated video clips, "commercial streaming video" describes collections of programs that are purchased through a vendor, primarily for educational use. Most of the videos are fairly short, and some are segments of longer video programs that have been selected to demonstrate a particular concept, show a specific event in history, or give information about a historical figure or celebrity. Several packages exist and can be purchased from vendors that specialize in this medium. As with electronic databases, the prices and scope of video collections will vary greatly. Search the Web for "streaming video" to find producers from which this resource can be purchased. Most collections are fairly expensive, so while streaming video can certainly be beneficial to teen customers, small libraries with limited budgets may not be able to afford this resource. Also, school districts will sometimes provide this service, so library staff should check with schools in their community before purchasing streaming video services.

Free Web Resources

While free Web sites can be an invaluable supplement to the library's collection, it is critical that library staff examine Web sites for accuracy and authority before making them available via bookmarks, as favorites on a computer, or as links on the library's Web site. Questions to ask when evaluating free web sites include the following:

- Who created the site? If the site's creator cannot be found or is discovered not to be authoritative, then that site should not be made accessible to teen customers. Look at the creator's credentials, including degrees earned, affiliations with professional organizations, and background and experience listed.
- Can the information included on the site be verified in other sources or does it simply consist of unauthorized claims made by the creator of the site?
- How often is the site updated? Just like the other material in a library, Web sites should be up to date and accurate.
- Is the site content rich or simply laden with interesting graphics?
- Is the site easy to navigate and attractively arranged?
- Is the site affiliated with a respected organization or company so that it will be active on a long-term basis?
- Does the information included on the site meet the selection criteria included in the library's collection policy?
- Is the site appropriate for the library's teen customers in terms of content, interest, and reading levels?

Downloadable Audio

Like streaming video, downloadable audio resources are usually composed of a collection of full-text books and music that can be accessed via an Internet-capable computer. Depending upon the licensing agreement with the vendor, these materials can usually be downloaded and played or viewed on such devices as CDs, MP3 players, or iPods™ for a certain period of time, after which they are automatically "checked in" and are no longer accessible. Downloadable movies are also available, and these differ from streaming video in that they are typically full-length, popular motion pictures. As with streaming video, downloadable audio/video can sometimes be quite expensive. Costs vary depending upon the size of the downloadable collection and other factors determined by vendors.

Virtual Collections

All of the above electronic resources may be a part of a library's virtual collection that can typically be accessed not only within the physical library but also from remote locations such as customers' homes or schools. Commonly, library customers will go to the library's Web site and must type in their name and library card number to gain access to the electronic resources provided. If the library's virtual collection is to be vital to teen and other customers, it should be arranged in some type of logical order, just like the physical collection. Thus, organizing the collection on the library's Web site by topic, subject, or format is necessary. While virtual collections are certainly an important part of the overall library collection, at present they will not totally replace the rest of the collection, as print books, magazines, and other items are still highly popular in most public libraries. However, virtual collections are growing in importance, and teen customers who may not regularly visit the library may be avid library users of these resources. In fact, a virtual collection could be a tool for enticing teens to actually visit the library. Since much of this collection requires the customer to login with a library card number, teens will have to visit the library at least once to obtain a card. This visit provides library staff with an excellent opportunity to show teens the other resources, programs, and services that are available only to customers coming into the library.

Internet and E-Mail

The Internet and e-mail are common resources in today's high-tech world. Therefore, library staff members will need to develop policies and procedures that govern the use of both resources and that are teen friendly but safe. Internet predators abound, so libraries need to be aware of the dangers and help educate parents and teens to ensure safety. These are certainly not easy issues with which to deal, so in order to get input from the community, asking an adult library advisory committee and teen library advisory committee to participate in the process is imperative! Such factors as how access will be provided, when the Internet and e-mail can be used, the purposes for which Internet and e-mail should be used, and how much time will be allowed for each customer to use computers for Internet or e-mail access will need to be discussed and decided upon, as well as the process and systems that will be put in place to inform customers of these policies and procedures.

Access to Material

Today's teens are busier than ever, so if, for example, the user logins to the library's electronic databases are not working when a teen customer needs access to them for an important school assignment, the chances of that teen ever using the databases again are slim. Teens are also reluctant to contact library staff and ask for help, so rather than calling attention to themselves, they will more than likely avoid using that particular library resource again. Since technological problems do indeed occur from time to time, the library should have in place an easy and nonthreatening process for teens to alert staff to these problems. Teen customers should be able to contact the library via e-mail to inform them of problems, and library staff should always respond in a timely manner, giving these customers an update on the status of the problem.

The same is true of print materials. If the most popular teen books are always checked out, then the librarian needs to purchase additional copies of the books or provide an easy process for teens to submit requests to hold a book when it is returned to the library or for staff to borrow the books from another library via interlibrary loan. The ideal situation would be for the library's automation software system to allow for electronic "patron-placed holds" in which a teen customer simply fills out a request for an item online and the automation system generates a holds slip that a staff member retrieves from the system so that the item can be located and held for the teen customer once it is returned. If it is not possible to place electronic requests and holds directly into the library automation software, then the library should provide some type of online form that can be filled out and submitted to library staff via e-mail. Once the e-mail form is received, the staff member should respond in a timely manner to let the teen customer know that the request has been received and is being processed.

WEB RESOURCES

Collection Development Policies, sponsored by the Arizona State Library: http://www. lib.az.us/cdt/colldev.htm—an excellent resource for assisting small libraries in developing and writing a collection development policy.

Collection Development Policy: Spokane Public Library: http://www.spokanelibrary. org/about/pdfs/Coll_Dev_Policy.pdf—a comprehensive collection development policy that covers all aspects of collection development and management, including the young adult collection.

Digital Library Collection Development Policy from the University of Texas at Austin: http://www.lib.utexas.edu/admin/cird/policies/subjects/framework.html—a model policy for those libraries who need information on developing and maintaining electronic collections.

Memorial Hall Library's Collection Development Manual 2005, Circulation Formats for the Young Adult Collection: http://www.mhl.org/about/policies/cd/formats/ya.htm—a guide to the selection of various types of materials for the young adult collection, along with selection sources and weeding guidelines.

Minneapolis Public Library: Library Board and Administration Collection Development Policy: http://www.mplib.org/cdp.asp—the collection development policy for this public library; an excellent brief model for policy development.

CHAPTER 4

Readers' Advisory

WHAT IS READERS' ADVISORY?

Simply put, readers' advisory means putting customers together with books (or other reading material) that they enjoy and want to read, that is, matching the right reader to the right book. Francis Bacon, in "Of Studies," from *Essays II,* stated that "Some books are to be tasted, others to be swallowed, and some few to be chewed and digested." As S. R. Ranganathan, the father of modern library science, put it in his five laws of library science, "Every person his book and every book its reader!" As a general rule, librarians truly believe these maxims, and not only do we relish books but many of us are, in fact, bibliophiles—basically book maniacs. Thus, we do not have to be convinced that books and reading are both very good things. However, this is not necessarily true of the teen customers with whom we come into contact—especially in today's world of generous, professionally rendered, high-tech graphics and small bits and bites of printed information that can be delivered to computers almost instantaneously and can be read within seconds. So, how then can we convince these reluctant book readers to use such antiquated technology as the lowly book?

This chapter will provide some suggestions for enticing teens to read, and yes, some of what they read may be in electronic format rather than between the covers of the traditional book. After all, the term is "readers' advisory" NOT "book readers' advisory." Keep that in mind as the following suggestions and ideas, some of which may be very different from standard approaches, are presented.

THE READERS' ADVISORY INTERVIEW

Although a readers' advisory interview can take the form of traditional book recommendations using a kind of "If you liked Harry Potter, you'll just LOVE..." approach, it may take different forms depending upon the type of reading material that library staff are promoting to teens. First, we should not assume that all teens love fiction and read only fiction for pleasure. Some teens may be avid fact hounds and read nonfiction books or other texts for enjoyment. One longtime librarian that the author knows personally claims she never reads fiction but is captivated by well-written nonfiction texts. To try to convince her that she should read the latest fantasy or romance novel is not only a waste of time but certainly would not have endeared her to the public library when she was a teen! Therefore, before librarians can recommend books or other reading material that a teen might enjoy, they must determine the teen's interests, that is, what fiction genres, nonfiction topics, various formats, and electronic texts the teen enjoys.

Doing this requires that library staff members ask questions, as in the reference interview process, and before they can begin to ask questions about the reading interests of teens, they should have established a credible relationship with the teens with whom they are working, as has been emphasized throughout this book. That means that members of the library staff must establish a trusting, open, friendly, responsive, respectful relationship between themselves and the teens they serve. Once this type of relationship is established, then staff members can engage in the readers' advisory interview process with their teen customers.

As mentioned previously, like the reference interview, the readers' advisory interview typically begins with questions. When a teen customer approaches a library staff member to ask for recommendations on books to read, the staff member can begin the interview by asking general questions and then moving to more specific questions. The sequence might progress like this:

Teen:	Do you have any good books that I could read?
Staff member:	Are you interested in reading a fiction book for pleasure, or do you prefer informational books?
Teen:	I want to find some really good fiction books to take on vacation with me. I'll be riding in the car for about four hours each way, so I need pretty thick books.
Staff member:	What kinds of books do you like—mysteries, fantasies, science fiction, or others?

Teen:	I like books about people who live in weird worlds and do strange things—not books about ordinary people.
Staff member:	Do you mean books like Harry Potter?
Teen:	Well, kind of like that but more like about kids who deal with strange creatures and stuff.
Staff member:	We have some graphic novels that you might like. Have you ever read any of these types of books?
Teen:	Yeah, but there's just not enough words in those books to keep me busy for four hours.
Staff member:	OK, what about books about magical, scary, or science fiction–type situations?
Teen:	That might work. What books would those be?
Staff member:	Well, this one, *Elsewhere* by Gabrielle Zevin, is about a girl who finds herself on a ship going to a place called Elsewhere where everyone ages backwards. It's pretty strange but very believable and full of surprises. This book called *Peeps* is about these kids who are vampires. Vampirism is a disease that can be caught simply by kissing. It's pretty graphic, so you'd need to decide whether you wanted a book with some violence in it. Here's another one you might like. It's *A Certain Slant of Light* by Laura Whitcomb, and it's about a girl who is a ghost who has haunted people for 130 years and is then "seen" by a teenage boy. They work together to figure out what happened to them in their pasts.
Teen:	Wow! Those all sound pretty good. I think I want the first one and the last one. Thanks!

Note that while the staff member does make some positive comments about each book, no heavy arm twisting is done to try to convince the teen to choose a specific book. Nor does the staff member tell the teen that because *she* liked the book, the teen will definitely like it too! The positive comments are more like (and, in fact could very well be) those that are included in critical reviews from professional journals, which will be discussed later in this chapter. Once the staff member begins to narrow down the topics and types of books in which the teen is interested to a few categories or genres, then, and only then, does the staff member select specific books to recommend.

After a readers' advisory interview is completed, the librarian should set up a file with each teen customer's name on a card or in an electronic database. The records should include the name of the teen customer, the date, the titles that were checked out, and, if possible, the feedback that the teen gave about each book after having read it. This will enable library staff to make recommendations for future books. However, just as adult reading tastes sometimes change, so do those of teens, so it is important to check with teens from time to time to find out whether they still like the same kinds of books. It is also good to gently guide teens to a wider variety of books to broaden their reading experiences whenever it is feasible. Again, this should not be done in a "convincing" mode but rather in a guiding, helpful way and *only* if the teen is responsive to this guidance. If not, let the teen customer read every horror book in your library, for example, and then be prepared to borrow additional ones from other libraries to continue to meet the customer's reading needs and interests!

OFFERING SUGGESTIONS IN SUCH A WAY THAT TEENS WILL RESPOND

If the relationship between a librarian and a teen customer is very good, it is much easier to make reading suggestions that teens will accept. However, even when the relationship is good, teen customers will still be resistant to the heavy-handed, preachy, "I loved it so you have to love it too!" type of pressure from staff members. Once in a while, a staff member and a teen may have such similar reading tastes and such a good relationship that this approach is feasible. More often than not, librarians need to use a softer approach, such as the one illustrated in the sample interview. If you have read the book, then you can certainly speak from a personal perspective. However, it is still important to state that this is strictly "my" opinion and it may not be "yours." Some readers' advisory purists have said that librarians should not make any comments, either positive or negative, when conducting a readers' advisory interview but should, instead, simply describe a book objectively and state the facts about it. This author does not agree with that philosophy. If you are not enthusiastic about the books you recommend to teens, it will be difficult to convince them to try out the titles you are recommending. Again, gentle guiding plus genuine interest in a book will go a long way toward encouraging teens to read a new book. Just as in other encounters with teen customers, their acceptance or rejection of a book you've recommended is not a personal acceptance or rejection, so it should not be taken personally.

If a teen rejects a book you have recommended, that does not mean that you have failed to present a strong case for the book. It simply means the teen is not interested in that particular book at that particular time. Depending, again, upon the staff member's relationship with a teen, it may be appropriate to recommend that same book at a future time, after the teen has perhaps read other books that are similar in nature, when the teen has reached a different reading or personal maturity level, or when events in the teen's life or in our society make the book a more popular choice. An example of the last-mentioned situation may be seen after a book has been made into a movie. At this point, some books that were previously "sleepers" or "shelf sitters" may suddenly become wildly popular! On the other hand, if a book or series of books gets too much exposure, to the point that it becomes passé, teen customers who might have read a book or series previously may now want nothing to do with it. Thus, librarians need not only to be aware of how teen customers' reading tastes are changing but also to be aware of how society, particularly in the teens' world, is changing and the implications those changes may have on teens' reading interests.

READERS' ADVISORY 2.0

Internet/Web 2.0 and its implications for research and information use are discussed in many conversations among today's librarians. But what about readers' advisory 2.0, in which librarians utilize high-tech, cutting-edge Web resources to enliven and revitalize readers' advisory services for teen customers? Librarians typically think of readers' advisory as putting customers together with books they will like. However, with the advent of Web-based resources and formats such as e-mail lists, blogs, iTunes™ playlists, wikis, podcasts, RSS feeds, *MySpace* pages, and others, readers' advisory has morphed into something much more sophisticated, and it continues to change as new technology-based tools become available.

If you are still limiting your library's readers' advisory services to teens to the traditional model, you may quickly see a decline in the number of teen customers who are using this service. Of course, we still want to recommend good books to teens, but we could do this in ways that are very different from traditional approaches. Also, sometimes the goal may simply be to get teens to read *something* rather than to entice them to read a print book. So what can be done to better ensure that teen readers' advisory is still a popular and demanded service in your library? The following are some ideas for conducting successful readers' advisory services and expanding the concept of readers' advisory so that this important service is used and appreciated by teens.

The first and most important requirement to keep readers' advisory alive and well in your library is, of course, always to be aware of the type of books your teen customers want to read. Although this has been mentioned previously, it is the most critical requirement for library staff and one that staff should actively pursue on a continuous basis. Some of the latest published studies on teen reading interests point to a shift in these interests. The studies indicate that teens' tastes have changed from reading contemporary, realistic fiction, including stories about "real" teens who look, behave, and sound like today's teenagers, complete with the same personal and social problems, to books about characters whose lives are very different from those of today's teens—think Harry Potter and *Eldest*.

If this is true of your teen customers, then rather than recommending the teenage angst classic *Catcher in the Rye* by J. D. Salinger, in which the protagonist Holden Caulfield's life and problems are very much like those of today's teens, you may want to recommend *Twilight and New Moon* by Stephanie Meyer, in which a teenage girl discovers that her new love interest and his entire family are vampires. Of course, by the time this book is available, teens' reading tastes may have dramatically changed, so it is important to stay abreast of the changes. Ideas for staying current in teen services and continuing to grow professionally are included in chapter 6. One of the simplest ways of finding out what your teen customers want is obviously just to ask them. If you have a teen advisory board, this group can help you and offer suggestions about both the types of books they want and also specific titles and authors that are popular.

So, you are excellent at staying on top of your teen customers' reading interests, but you still can't seem to keep teens motivated to read the books you are recommending. What next? Some teens have different motivations for engaging in text than just wanting to read "a good book." They may want to delve into the authors' lives and get to know them on a more personal basis. They may want to find out what type of music an author likes or even recommend some cool music to their favorite author. They may want to see and hear their favorite author in "real time" or get updates about what's going on in an author's life. They may want to share ideas and information with other teens who share the same reading tastes or favorite authors. Or they may just want to interact with the text in a way that simply reading a book does not allow. For these teen customers, librarians will need to use a variety of resources and strategies to encourage them to read and appreciate books.

Many young adult (teen) authors have their own Web sites, so this approach to reaching young readers is not unusual. However, a growing trend among authors is also to provide readers with ways to interact with them via their Web sites so that communication is now two way between authors and their audiences. This high-tech book promotion takes many forms and is limited only by the imaginations of the authors themselves and the way they feel about being more intimate with their readers. Authors have incorporated on their Web sites techniques such as the following: fully animated videos, podcast trailers, or book talks by the authors to introduce their new books; reviews written by teens; discographies of music to accompany the text of their books; playlists of the authors' favorite music, sometimes allowing teens to download or add to the playlists; interactive blogs on which teen customers can post messages to the authors or to other teen readers; e-mail discussion lists to which teens can sign on; wikis providing additional information about books; expanded and interactive reading formats in which readers can ask questions about a book and present their answers or theories; and authors' journals. Authors also sponsor forums on social networking sites such as the *MySpace* group for Teen Lit, which currently has approximately 500 members.

Librarians can use some or all of these resources to promote books and reading or simply to introduce teen readers to the various authors and genres of fiction that are available. In fact, some teen readers may never actually read an entire book but instead derive reading pleasure from engaging in interactive discussion groups that are available via the Web. It is this type of readers' advisory that may not fit the traditional model; nevertheless, if the goal is to get teens to read, then *what* they read is not nearly as important as the fact that they *are* reading! Thus, librarians can provide access to these sites and services on the library's Web site so that they are available from home, but also provide follow-up programming that is available only in the library, in order to keep teen customers visiting the library as well. Such programming will be discussed in chapter 5. The plethora of tools that are available via the Web make readers' advisory services much more exciting and vibrant than past approaches, and librarians can be the means for today's teens to gain information and assistance in using these tools in ever-changing ways to keep teens reading and using the library!

BIBLIOTHERAPY

Simply put, bibliotherapy means using books to help people, specifically teens, solve problems. Despite the fact that some people in the library science field have argued that bibliotherapy is no longer a viable tool to use with today's teens, this author feels that is not the case. It does seem accurate to state that books cannot "heal" teens who have social or psychological problems or be used to "treat" those problems or even to "solve" them. Nonetheless, books can indeed provide some comfort and reassurance for teens who are struggling with serious issues and may have difficulty in understanding how to cope with serious situations in their personal lives. The idea that "I am not in this alone" is a powerful concept with which to help teens see beyond their individual struggles and realize that they do not need to feel alienated from the rest of the world. Thus, librarians who have knowledge of teens' personal situations can bring to bear books that are appropriate to assist teens with these situations.

Despite the fact that you may have knowledge of a teen's personal problems, be aware that a great deal of sensitivity is necessary when you recommend books that address these problems. Teens may feel threatened by knowing that you know their situation. In this case, they may avoid you or avoid returning to the library due to embarrassment or discomfort. Thus, use caution and proceed slowly when attempting to implement bibliotherapy with a teen customer. It may be wise to recommend a variety of books, some of which include the problems or issues the teen is facing, and some of which do not. Then, if teens read the "blurb" on each book, they can readily see that not all of the books address their situation, and this may make them feel slightly less threatened. Parents, too, will sometimes feel threatened if they are aware that the librarian has recommended a book on alcoholism in the family, for example, so it is important to remember not to violate the privacy of your teen customers' reading preferences by discussing the books they are reading with anyone else. Once teens realize that you can be trusted in this way, they will be much more likely to be open and honest in revealing issues and situations with which they are struggling.

Chapter 1 included a list of teen issues of which librarians need to be aware. Librarians can use this list as a starting place from which to select books that feature characters who are dealing with these issues. Note that some authors specialize in writing about teen issues and problems, so it will be helpful to keep a file of these authors and the topics about which they write. Also, remember that many teens read adult books rather than limiting their reading to books labeled "young adult" fiction. Therefore, do not restrict your recommendations to young adult (YA) fiction, as many adult fiction books will also include teen characters who are struggling with issues and problems. In fact, there seems to be a growing trend to include teen characters in books that are written for adults, so it will not be difficult to find this type of material for your teen customers.

ADULT BOOKS FOR TEENS

As has just been noted, many authors include teen characters in their books, as well as topics and situations in their plots that are of interest to teens. Some teens, in fact, may exclusively read adult books rather than those fiction books designated "young adult." Angelina Benedetti, a teen librarian, states that when she was a teen, she would only have read YA fiction if someone had coerced her to do so! Benedetti (2004) goes on to say that since she is now selecting teen materials for her library, she does indeed read teen literature. However, the message here is clear. Some teens do not want to be limited to the teen fiction collection. Therefore, librarians should consider the impact of such teenagers' preferences on how books are selected for libraries, who selects books for teens, which books to use for book talks, which titles to recommend in readers' advisory interviews, and even perhaps where the teen collection should be located (or whether duplicate copies of some adult books should be shelved in the teen collection).

How to Select

When selecting or recommending adult books for teens, give consideration to the following questions:

- Are teen characters included in a book? This is not always a requirement, but it can sometimes heighten teens' interest in reading a particular adult book.
- Does the author present developmental stages or tasks to which teens will relate? Examples are struggling for independence from parents or other authority figures; deciding what is right or wrong; dealing with a first romantic relationship; forming close friendships with peers or adults; or developing a belief system in the areas of politics, social issues, personal integrity, religion, and others. Teens can quickly relate to emotional states and intellectual decisions or challenges that are familiar to their age group, as well as problems and issues that teenagers encounter.
- Can the book be read on different levels? This will enable teen readers to "get" the author's meaning without dealing with some of the more adult-focused issues and the emotions to which older readers may pay more attention.
- Are there universal themes or recognizable character types in the book with which all readers can identify? Teens are so peer impacted that they may not appreciate a book in which the theme is esoteric or the characters truly do not reflect any recognizable personality traits.

- Does the author include relationships and conflicts with which teens are familiar, for example, human vs. human, human vs. nature, human vs. the forces of evil, human vs. society?
- Are other books by the same author appealing to teen customers? Some authors of adult novels such as Stephen King have track records of writing adult books that teens relish. Learn who these authors are, and you will have a steady stream of adult books to recommend to your teen customers.

Some other tools to help you select adult books popular with teens are teen choice lists developed for various states' reading programs, teen recommendations that can easily be solicited via a suggestion box in your teen library, YA-oriented Web sites that list good reads for teens, authors' Web sites, lists of teen books developed by other public libraries and available on the Web, and the numerous lists of recommended and award-winning books for teens on YALSA's Web site. The URLs for several of these resources are given in the Web Resources section at the end of this chapter.

What to Avoid

Several items should raise red flags when you are selecting adult books to recommend to teens. Although most of these are simply logical considerations, it is always good to review them from time to time.

- Avoid recommending books that address topics not of interest to teens, such as those featuring older females dealing with menopause or novels that deal with the world of business.
- Avoid recommending books in which teens are stereotyped, put down, or shown in a negative light.
- Avoid didactic or preachy-sounding books in which the teen characters are continually berated by their "I told you so" elders.
- Avoid recommending books that portray teen characters as idealistic, perfect, super children.
- Also avoid recommending books that portray families as idealistic or perfect.
- Avoid recommending books that are watered down and present a perfect world—unless the books are dealing with some type of futuristic, science fiction–type new order, for example.
- Avoid recommending simplistic, formulaic books, as teens will become just as bored with these as adult readers are.
- Finally, avoid recommending adult books to teens just because they are on some kind of best seller list.

It is important that you are familiar with the content of the adult books you recommend to teens via reading reviews, lists of recommendations created by professional organizations or teens themselves, or recommendations from your peers.

MINI BOOK TALKS

School librarians sometimes have opportunities to conduct book talks or author talks for extended periods of time when classroom teachers bring their students to the school library. Public library staff may not have these kinds of opportunities, outside of planned author visits or meetings of teen book clubs. What public library staff members do have opportunities to present are abbreviated, sound bite–type book talks when working with teens one on one or in small groups. Thus, librarians should be prepared to give brief talks about new fiction books of interest to teens. This does not mean that librarians need to have read the books from cover to cover. It does mean that librarians who work with teens need at least to be familiar enough with a book to be able to read or recite short sections that will make the book appealing to teen customers.

Since you will probably not be able to memorize these mini book talks or remember which books have specific plots or characters, it is helpful to keep a card file with titles of books, authors' names, and brief summaries of each book. You may not need to give an overview of the entire plot and should not, in fact, give away the endings. What you will want to do is give teen customers a taste of what the book is about and perhaps read one or two sentences that are particularly enticing. These "grabber" lines may be enough to encourage teen customers to read the book without knowing more about the plot. Each book will have its own unique quality, and with experience, you will quickly find out what works and what doesn't when delivering a mini book talk to a teen customer.

If you do not have time to create and maintain a card file of fiction books in the teen collection, this task could be delegated to teens who belong to a library book club, teen advisory club members, or teen volunteers. Note: be sure that teens who help with this project have a real passion for the books about which they are writing. In fact, if you can assign specific titles to teens who are avid readers in a particular genre, science fiction buffs, for example, the descriptions they create for the card file will be much more interesting. Also, consider posting these reviews on the teen pages of your library's Web site rather than keeping hard copies in a card file. Then teen customers will have ready access to them so that a staff member need not be available. However, if part of your goal is to establish good relationships with teen customers, you may want to have a few really "hot" titles that you "book talk" in person to teens.

FORMATS AND TYPES OF BOOKS

To be able to match the right book with the right teen customer, you must be familiar with the various kinds of books that are available for this group. Just as individual teens prefer certain genres of fiction, they will also want or need particular types of books that match their reading levels and interests. Also, the use to which the books are put—whether reading for pleasure, for homework, or for research—may restrict the choices to a specific type of book. As you conduct a readers' advisory interview, it will be important for you to know about various formats and types of books, as well as how the books will be used, so that you can make recommendations that are both pleasing to teen customers and suitable to meet their specific needs.

In addition to knowing about the formats for various categories of teen books, you must also be familiar with the shelving arrangements for the teen collection. For example, although graphic novels would appear to be most suitably shelved in the fiction section of the library, the Library of Congress catalog records, which are typically adhered to in many libraries, classify graphic novels in the same section of the library as cartoon books such as those based on the Peanuts or Garfield comic strips, that is, in the 700s in the Dewey Decimal Classification System. Thus, these books may actually be shelved in the nonfiction section of your library. Some formats and types of books that are included in a typical teen collection are discussed below.

Picture Books for Older Readers

Although we typically tend to think of these books as being "easy" books for younger readers, many of the picture books that are published today are quite complex and sophisticated, both in their illustrations and in their content. Therefore, some teen library collections may include books in this format. Some of these books may be similar to the typical, 32-page picture book, with full-page illustrations, but the plots, characters, settings, and themes may be such that they are appealing to and more appropriate for older children and sometimes even adults. Classroom teachers at the middle school and high school levels sometimes use these books with their students, for example, to teach the elements of literature, provide ideas for writing projects, and examine various art media. The teen library staff can partner with the children's services library staff to help identify specific titles of books in this category and make them available to teens.

Fiction

Fiction books for teens can take many forms, including young adult fiction books that are specifically written for this age group, adult novels that are appealing to and appropriate for teens, diaries or journals of various characters or fictionalized diaries of historical figures, books written in free verse, which are becoming more and more popular due to their sparse text, series fiction in which stories are continued and the same main characters are featured in each volume, edgy books that push the limits due to graphic content or controversial themes, books from which movies or TV shows are created, and many others. Some teens will have specific preferences in fiction reading and may read fiction books only of a specific genre, such as mystery or science fiction, while other teens' reading tastes will be more eclectic. Thus, teen library staff will need to become well versed in the multitude of types of fiction that are available in their library. The various types of genre fiction will be described later in this chapter.

Serial Fiction

Think Stephen King's *Green Mile* and you will have a basic understanding of this format. King's serial novel, which was written in six parts, and others like it can be highly popular for teens who are just beginning to read fiction, are struggling readers, do not have much time to read for pleasure, or simply enjoy this format. The difference between series fiction and serial fiction is that in series fiction, each title can stand alone, as the story comes to a conclusion or resolution, while in serial fiction, the story is "to be continued" in the next book. Basically, serial fiction can be compared to the long chapters of a book that have been divided into separate volumes. Sometimes all of the volumes comprising a serial fiction novel are shorter than a full-length traditional novel. Thus, they may be more popular among those teens who struggle to complete a young adult or adult novel. These types of books are also similar in nature to TV shows that continue from week to week, so this is a familiar format to teen library users.

Multicultural and International Fiction

Whether your community is homogeneous or very diverse in its racial and ethnic populations, you will want to provide some multicultural and international fiction books for your teen customers. Technology and lightning-fast communication systems have provided teens with much more information and therefore more curiosity and interest in people who may be different from themselves. Today's teens have a much better understanding and appreciation of learning about those different from themselves, and the list of excellent international or non-Anglo authors continues to grow.

In the past, while some titles written by Anglo American authors about people of different racial or ethnic groups in the United States or from other countries were very well written, many did not authentically reflect the racial and ethnic groups of whom they were supposed to be representative. They had been Americanized, so to speak. Sometimes books about Asians, for example, were written by Anglo American authors who, while they developed interesting plots, may not have known much about their subjects. Thus, the characters seemed stilted, social problems were contrived, and erroneous cultural assumptions were made.

This is no longer the case. In fact, books written by non-Americans or non-Anglo Americans are becoming widely available and are growing in popularity among teens. One need only look at the titles and authors of recent award-winning and highly praised books for children and teens to realize that this is true. Several of the recent Newbery Medal winners and runners up or "honor" books written for older children, such as the 2005 winner *Kira Kira* by Cynthia Kadohata and the 2002 winner *A Single Shard* by Linda Sue Park, are representative of this trend. For teens, the 2007 Michael L. Printz award winner, *American Born Chinese* by Gene Luen Yang, and *Black Juice,* a 2006 Printz Honor Book by Australian author Margo Lanagan, are excellent examples of books written by non-Anglo American authors who have achieved honor and gained popularity among today's teens. Librarians who work with teens will want to continually seek these types of books for teen collections so that teen customers can continue to learn about and appreciate people, places, and cultures different from their own.

High/Low Books

High/low books are books that are written on topics of high interest to older children but with an easier vocabulary and reading level. They are appropriate for either struggling or reluctant readers; and they come in many varieties, from easy fiction or graphic novels to easy nonfiction books. Note: when selecting high/low books, library staff must be aware that some of these books are very unappealing to teens due to cover art, plot lines, or simply the fact that they are "skinnier" than teen or adult novels. Careful selection is mandatory for this type of book. Otherwise, the high/low books will be shelf sitters that teens will avoid for fear of looking or feeling foolish among their peers. Some publishers specialize in this type of book. The *High/Low Handbook* by Libretto and Barr (2002) is an excellent resource for selecting high/low books for teens. See the bibliography for complete information on this resource.

Graphic Novels

First, it is important to note that graphic novels are a format, NOT a genre of fiction. These books are indeed typically fiction, but they, like serial fiction, represent a particular format and style in which the stories are written, rather than a particular genre. In fact, graphic novels can cover a multitude of genres including mystery, horror, science fiction, and others. These books are similar in nature to the comic book format in that they have sparse text and generous graphical content, often presented in panes with speech balloons for various characters. However, graphic novels are usually much lengthier than comic books, hence the term "novels," and can often stand as complete works rather than being serialized with characters who continue to be involved throughout the series. On the other hand, some graphic novels can and do include several volumes in a series, but these are typically still much longer works than traditional comic books, with more complex plots. Although graphic novels are so named because of their graphically rich presentation, some are indeed also graphic in terms of sexual content and violence. Thus, some titles may not be appropriate for younger teens and 'tweens. More information on this format is included in chapter 3.

Nonfiction

Although we sometimes tend to think of nonfiction as being used strictly for homework assignments or research projects, some teens, just like adults, prefer to read informational texts for pleasure. Sometimes reluctant or struggling readers prefer nonfiction books because they feature generous, full-color illustrations with bulleted lists or brief paragraphs of text rather than the lengthy narratives that are found in fiction books. Also, some nonfiction books are similar in appearance to Web sites and this makes them appealing to teens who are computer buffs, love surfing the Web, and like smaller bits of text to read. In fact, unless your library has plenty of computers at which teens can access many online databases, you may need to provide backup print copies of some nonfiction books such as those in the Opposing Viewpoints series, which is used very frequently for science or social studies reports and debate-type speeches, as well as print copies of nonfiction reference material that may not yet be available online or is too expensive to purchase. In fact, you will need to weigh the cost of providing extensive online databases against the cost of print materials, to decide which format is appropriate for your library. Typically, libraries will provide a mixture of print and online nonfiction and reference resources. However, since many of today's teens greatly prefer a digitized format, the more online resources your library can provide, the better.

Teens that are mechanically oriented may enjoy and use how to do it–type handbooks or manuals such as the *Chilton Auto Repair Manuals*. While these are available online as a subscription database, as with other online resources, the costs could be prohibitive. Thus, this resource may need to be available via print books, or alternatively, back issues in print could be maintained and the online version purchased as the budget permits. Basically, nonfiction books can be used in many ways for a multitude of purposes, and may, in fact, be preferred over fiction books by some teen customers. Therefore, when conducting a readers' advisory interview, library staff should remember to ask whether a teen customer prefers fiction or nonfiction before recommending specific books.

GENRES OF FICTION

On Libraries Unlimited's Genreflecting Web site, based on the series of books by Diana Tixier Herald, genre fiction is described as stories that have a particular (recognized) type of story and content and are written in a certain style (Libraries Unlimited 2004). Certain conventions define and describe the various genres, such as specific locations and time periods (settings) in which stories take place, types of characters, and particular types of roles and relationships. Genre fiction is very plot intensive, with specific elements of the plot being incorporated into each type of genre.

For example, in the mystery genre, readers are presented with an unsolved murder or some other crime or puzzle that begs to be solved for the story to be resolved in a satisfactory way. In the romance genre, there is, of course, a "boy meets girl" type of plot upon which the story is based. In horror books, the plot involves horrific events or circumstances. The reader is typically presented with a plot that addresses good vs. evil, with the evil being represented in the form of some horrific being or force such as those that are ubiquitous in Stephen King's books. The adventure/survival genre typically includes a protagonist or protagonists faced with some type of conflict such as human vs. nature or human vs. human, in which they must struggle to survive. Characters in these stories are generally doing things or traveling to places that are out of the norm for most people, or they are placed in situations with which most people do not have to deal. Historical fiction is, of course, based on some event(s) from the past. Thus, genre fiction is usually very recognizable by the reader due to its plot elements and, to some extent, its character types.

Many teens prefer to read books in only one or two genres and will seldom stray from their preferred genres. Librarians will quickly become familiar with these teens' reading preferences as they seek titles by the same author or small group of authors. There are several options for addressing the issue of the one-genre teen reader:

1.   You can simply continue to direct these teens to authors and titles in the genre they prefer. The challenge here is that you may not have enough books in the genre to be able to continue to meet a particular teen's reading needs. If this is the case, be prepared to borrow books from other libraries via interlibrary loan services. Also, if your goal is to create lifelong readers who will continue to mature in their reading abilities and tastes, you will not be able to meet this goal by continuing to direct the teen to the same genre and authors all of the time.

2.   You can use the Amazon-like approach to readers' advisory with the teen to at least introduce him to new authors in the genre or gradually move him to a similar genre in the hope of helping him to expand his reading repertoire. This entails an approach of this type: "If you liked _____ [supply the title], then you may want to try _____." Or "If you like _____'s books, then you may like _____'s books also."

3.   You can try to convince the teen to change genres by talking about the merits of a new book in a different genre. The interview would go something like this: "John, I know that you really like science fiction because you've pretty much read every science fiction book in our collection, as well as most of the science fiction books in the nearby libraries. Science fiction is really a pretty difficult genre to read, so I'm sure you could tackle just about any book you wanted at this point. Would you like to try something new for a change?" If the answer is "yes," then this will give you the perfect opportunity to introduce the teen to a different genre. Start with a genre that is similar to the one the teen typically

reads, moving from science fiction to fantasy, perhaps. If the answer is "no," then you might want to respond by saying, "OK, we'll stick with science fiction books. However, you may want to be thinking about trying a different type of book pretty soon because I'm quickly running out of good science fiction books for you to read. Perhaps next time you visit the library, I'll give you a list of books that are a bit different for you to try. Will this work for you?" Most teens would not be threatened or turned off by this soft approach, so even tentative agreement at this point would give you a license to begin to move the teen to a different genre.

The labels, groupings, and definitions of various genres of fiction vary greatly from one source to another. Thus, the information that is presented below, although similar to what is found in some sources, may be slightly different from what is found in others. Keep in mind that many of the genres are quite broad and can include a multitude of subgenres. For example, the fantasy genre includes such subgenres as Arthurian fantasy, dark fantasy, heroic fantasy, epic fantasy, and the list goes on! What this means in terms of readers' advisory is that even if you know what genre a teen customer prefers, you may need to continue to ask questions to find out what specific types of books within the genre the customer really wants to read. Asking additional questions such as the following will be helpful: "OK, Tom, you said that you really like fantasy books. Do you prefer fantasy based on legends such as the King Arthur–type fantasy books, sword and sorcery tales, modern fantasy, or some other type of fantasy book?" Of course, library staff members who provide readers' advisory services to teens will need to be well versed in the numerous genres and subgenres in order to be able to recommend books effectively to teens. Resources are plentiful, so all that is required is to spend some time reading reviews of books as well as the excellent resources that are available for library staff to become fluent in "genre speak." Once teen patrons realize that you are a genre expert and can be relied upon to provide accurate information about various books, they will truly value and appreciate your opinions and recommendations.

A list of genres and definitions follow. Subgenres may or may not be included, but these can easily be found in the free Web resources provided at the end of this chapter or in some of the excellent works included in the bibliography. At the end of each genre description is a list of authors who write in that genre. Some are authors of teen fiction. Others are authors of adult fiction that is popular with teens. Some authors' works are considered classics, and others are newer. These lists can be used as a starting point from which you can develop your own lists of recommended authors and titles for your teen customers. Once the lists have been developed, they will, of course, need to be kept up to date. Lists such as these can be used in a variety of ways—for staff to prepare book orders, for signage, as posters, on bookmarks, in card files of book reviews, on the library's teen Web site, for teen book clubs, in your library newsletter (electronic or hard copy) and in many other ways. The library's teen advisory board and teen customers will be able to suggest additional authors and titles, as well as helping you find ways to use the lists of authors and titles to promote the library's teen collection.

Fantasy

This genre includes stories about people, places, creatures, and events that are "fantastical" and supernatural. Although the tales are impossible to believe, good fantasy books are written so well that the reader will suspend disbelief and be mentally transported to the land in which the story occurs. Stories of magic, strange folks, past or future times, fairy tales, tales of mystical lands, myths, hero tales, and stories of magical creatures abound in this genre. Creatures such as wizards, witches, fairies, knights, kings and queens, sorcerers, trolls, dragons, unicorns, elves, and a multitude of other imaginary characters and creatures populate the fantasy genre. Examples of popular fantasy book series are the Harry Potter books by J. K. Rowling, the *Ring Trilogy* by J.R.R. Tolkien, and the *Inheritance Trilogy* by teen author Christopher Paolini. Other authors who write in this genre are Garth Nix, Kenneth Oppel, Tamora Pierce, and Lynne Abbey.

Science Fiction

Science fiction and fantasy share some traits: both may include imaginary characters and creatures and be set in imaginary places. However, science fiction differs from fantasy in that science fiction typically poses questions that make the reader think about the possibilities posed by real or imaginary scientific hypotheses. Some science fiction books can be quite dark, without the "happily ever after" endings that readers expect in the fairy tales included in the fantasy genre. Science fiction presents future societies in which the social rules, technology, physical environment, and other aspects of the setting are very different from our own. Such topics as alien life, time or space travel, utopian societies, robots, human engineering and cloning, bizarre governmental structures, supernaturally powerful humans and other creatures, and nuclear holocausts are included in this genre. Some well-known science fiction authors are Isaac Asimov, Robert A. Heinlein, Andre Norton, Neil Gaiman, George Orwell, and Arthur C. Clarke. This genre continues to evolve and grow; so many excellent titles are currently available.

Contemporary Realistic Fiction

Called by other names, such as realistic fiction, contemporary mainstream fiction, and contemporary fiction, for example, this genre includes stories that are set at the present time in today's world, feature characters that are like the girl or boy next door (or the teen readers themselves), and have plots about situations and events that could actually occur. This genre describes the types of human experiences and emotions that are considered to be universal in nature. Relationships are between such people as teens and parents or other authority figures, boyfriends and girlfriends, teachers and students, siblings, best friends, and strangers. Sometimes characters are presented with moral or ethical choices with which most of us are familiar, and the plots address the way the characters deal with their decisions. Some popular authors of adult or teen novels who write in this genre are Ellen Hopkins, An Na, Chris Crutcher, Lois Lowry (who also writes in other genres), Toni Morrison, Anne Tyler, and Pat Conroy.

Humor

Books in this genre are, of course, intended to be amusing. However, as straightforward as this may seem, because different people have different ideas of what is humorous, writers who are successful in this genre must be able to present situations, characters, and plots that are universal in nature, similar to those in the contemporary realistic fiction genre. In fact, humor is really more of a super genre, in the sense that humorous books or books with humorous elements can be found across the genres. However, some fiction books are written specifically to amuse the reader so that the primary purpose of the book is to induce joy and laughter. Thus, some books, despite the additional genre into which they may fit (such as fantasy or mystery), can be considered to fit within the humor category. Examples of books that fit into this genre as well as another genre are *The Hitchhiker's Guide to the Galaxy* by Douglas Adams (science fiction), *The Earth, My Butt, and Other Big Round Things* by Carolyn Mackler (contemporary realistic fiction), and Janet Evanovich's series of numbered mystery books starting with *One for the Money* (mystery).

Mystery and Suspense

Crimes, criminals, cliff-hanging danger, and solutions characterize this genre. Typically a policeman, FBI/CIA agent, private investigator, heroic private citizen, or some other kind of detective is involved in investigating a crime and seeking a solution or righting a wrong. Clues are presented throughout the book, and readers are typically enticed to try to solve the crime before the solution is presented. Suspense novels also usually present a crime of some kind, so they are closely akin to the mystery genre, but they may be faster paced and engage the reader in a life or death struggle of some kind. Examples of popular authors in these genres are Agatha Christie, Mickey Spillane, Lillian Jackson Braun, Lois Duncan, Alane Ferguson, and Joan Lowry Nixon.

Horror

Horrific monsters, whether real or imagined, are the hallmark of this genre. Thus, books in the genre are readily identifiable. The monsters in horror books can take many forms: they may be animal, vegetable, human, or simply monsters of the mind.

In addition to monsters, the horror genre usually features a struggle between good and evil, and books in this genre do not always have a happy ending. Some books, in fact, may leave the reader with unfinished business to deal with, when more open endings are included. Within this genre are numerous subgenres including those dealing with ghosts, vampires, werewolves, haunted houses, human maniacs such as serial killers, rabid or rampant animals, mummies and zombies, and any number of other imaginable or unimaginable terrifying creatures or places. Popular horror authors include the master of the genre, Stephen King, and also Dean Koontz, Clive Barker, Anne Rice, Stephanie Meyer, and Scott Westerfeld.

Adventure/Survival

Exotic locales, extreme hardships, limited resources, and resourceful people populate the works in the adventure/survival genre. Action and conflict are elements of this genre so that plots are fast paced and suspenseful. The action usually involves taking bold steps in order to survive, and some type of conflict with which the protagonist must deal. The conflicts included can be one or more of several types: human vs. nature, human vs. human, and others. Authors use the device of including a memorable yet vulnerable protagonist who must struggle to overcome life-threatening odds or address a difficult challenge, so that readers will identify with the character and be drawn into the story. Authors of adventure/survival books include Jack London, Dale Brown, Gary Paulsen, Mel Odom, and Will Hobbs.

Chick Lit

The chick lit genre is basically composed of books that will appeal to teen girls and young women, based, of course, upon the supposition that all young females have similar tastes in reading. Chick lit books are typically authored by women and feature young, hip women as the main characters. Plots address such real-life issues as romantic love, dating, marriage, friendships with peers, fashion trends, family life, social cliques, school or work environments, weight or eating disorders, and others. However, some books in this genre present situations or social environments to which readers may aspire, such as elite clubs or sororities or the high-fashion, high-society scene. Most of the books in this genre are written in a personal and even confidential tone, and some take the form of journals or diaries such as *Bridget Jones' Diary* and *The Princess Diary*. Well-known authors in this genre are Meg Cabot, Cecily von Ziegersar, Sonya Sones, Ann Brashares, Megan Shull, and Helen Fielding.

Urban Street Lit

Also known as urban, street, hip hop, or ghetto lit, such elements as in-your-face language, drugs, rap music, sex, and crime or violence characterize this genre.

The concept of the "mean streets" is exemplified, and often gang life and its consequences are presented. Books in this genre tend to be more graphic in nature than some other, more traditional types of fiction. Young protagonists are frequently presented with situations that require them to make life-changing decisions, and they are often victims of people, social institutions, or societal circumstances over which they have little or no control, such as gang violence, school authorities, law enforcement officials, prejudice, bullying and physical abuse from peers or parents, substance abuse, or a combination of these elements. Authors who write in this genre include Walter Dean Myers, Coe Booth, Lynne Ewing, and Sharon G. Flake.

Historical Fiction

Historical fiction is typically based on a particular event or set in a specific period in prehistory or history. Thus, the setting, that is, the time and place, is a critical component of this genre. While characters do not have to be based on real people, sometimes historical figures are included, but the speech or actions of these figures may or may not be factual. Both plots and characters can indeed be "fictionalized" to make for a more enjoyable or interesting read. Historical fiction can sometimes act as a catalyst, enticing teens to read actual nonfiction history books. Thus, it is a good idea to have informational books on some of the time periods and real people that are featured in historical novels. Authors of books in this genre include James Michener, James Clavell, Jean Auel, Carolyn Meyer, Mark Twain, Ann Rinaldi, Scott O'Dell, and James Collier.

Christian Fiction

Books in the Christian fiction genre appear to have been rapidly expanding recently, and although many titles are not specifically written for teens, as with most of the other genres, books in this category are becoming increasingly popular among members of this age group. Christian fiction covers a broad spectrum of other genres. While Christian fiction typically includes characters who practice the Christian religion and themes related to spiritual or religious life, plots can include almost anything characteristic of the other genres, such as mystery, crime, romance, friendship, fantasy or folktale, and others. What sets the genre apart is, of course, its emphasis on the Christian faith and the relationship between God and humankind, particularly the protagonist in each book. Authors include C. S. Lewis, Janette Oake, James Beau-Seigneur, Andrew M. Greeley, Richard Paul Evans, and Frank Peretti.

Westerns

Western fiction stories are typically set in the American West during the late nineteenth century, and they feature protagonists who are rough and tough cowboys (or girls), outlaws, or the law enforcement officials who are trying to bring the bad guys to justice. Some books include such famous historical figures as Billy the Kid, Wyatt Earp, or the Jesse James gang, and while these were indeed "real people," their characters may be fictionalized to better fit within the plots. Set in the past, Western fiction is similar in nature to historical fiction although it is limited to a specific time period and includes plots, settings, and characters reflective of that period. Since we have many historical records available, it is critical that Westerns are authentic with regard to the period and settings described. Due to the urbanization of America, this genre may not be as popular with some teens as genres that better reflect urban life. However, it is still a viable genre and one that librarians can introduce to teen customers who like mystery and suspense or adventure/survival fiction, since similar elements are included in all three of these genres. Authors who write in this genre are Zane Grey, Louis L'Amour, Larry McMurtry, and Loren D. Estelman.

Romance

Although this genre could be considered a subgenre of chick lit, because it primarily deals with one convention of that genre, romantic love, romance fiction stands alone. Books in this genre feature romantic relationships, or love stories, between two main characters, and they present these relationships in such a way as to encourage the reader to vicariously experience the emotions present within the relationships. The romance genre has long been popular with teen girls, but some of today's romance fiction is being written to appeal to teen boys.

Examples of romance fiction written specifically to entice teen boys are *Street Love* by Walter Dean Myers and *Nick and Norah's Infinite Playlist* by Rachel Cohn and David Levithan. *Street Love* is a story about two African American kids in Harlem who fall in love. It is a kind of modern Romeo and Juliet story written for guys. *Nick and Norah's Infinite Playlist* is about two music-obsessed teens who come together through a quirk of circumstance, spend an entire Saturday night traveling around New York City's clubs, and are forced to deal with the awkward first-date emotions that are so painfully familiar to teens. In addition to traditional romantic relationships, some books in this genre address homosexual romantic relationships. One example is *Boy Meets Boy* by David Levithan. Some teen boys may not want to be identified with the romance genre, so when you work with them, it might be more effective to refer to the genre as relationship fiction or give it some other, less obvious label. Other authors who write in this genre are Laura Whitcomb, Olive Ann Burns, Edith Pattou, Nicholas Sparks, Rachel Vail, and Jenny Han.

READING ALOUD TO TEENS

Although we tend to think of younger children and "story time" when the topic of reading aloud is mentioned, it is definitely appropriate to read aloud to teens as well.

In fact, read aloud sessions can provide a powerful motivator to teens who may be reluctant or struggling readers, to entice them to begin to read or help them to feel at ease when their peers are discussing books they have read. The venue is nonthreatening, and all it takes to make teen read alouds happen are a comfortable space where teens can sit and relax, knowledge of the literature that will be of interest to teens, and a person who possesses the ability to read with good expression and enthusiasm. The reader could be a library staff member, a parent or community volunteer, or a teen customer. Teen read alouds can be used as a readers' advisory tool from time to time, especially when new books lend themselves to read alouds, but these sessions can also be incorporated in the library's list of ongoing programs for teens. Here are some powerful benefits of reading aloud to teens;

- It provides quality time together for teen customers and library staff or volunteers.
- It helps teens develop their imaginations or creative thinking skills.
- It allows an opportunity for sharing or teaching values and social norms.
- It is an inexpensive form of high-quality entertainment.
- It provides an opportunity for busy teens to take some "down time."
- It helps establish better relationships between teens and library staff.
- It sparks discussions on topics of mutual interest.
- It gives staff an opportunity to learn more about teens' likes, dislikes, and reading tastes.
- It helps teens develop reading skills through hearing language.
- It helps teens develop listening skills and higher-order (critical) thinking skills.
- It provides a way to promote nonfiction books to teens who prefer informational text (obviously, the reader would not read an entire nonfiction book but might read brief excerpts from several nonfiction books that address similar topics).
- It provides a safe, comfortable environment for teen customers who might otherwise have no place to go after school hours.

TOOLS AND RESOURCES

Review Journals

Many professional journals for librarians include reviews of books for teens. Among these are *Booklist, School Library Journal, VOYA* (*Voice of Youth Advocates*), and *Library Media Connection.* These journals include articles of interest to those working in the library profession, as well as a generous number of reviews, written by librarians, teachers, and others who work in the publishing or library field. Some of the reviews provide ratings or recommendations, and all give an appropriate reading level, interest level, or both.

Subscription Databases

Two excellent resources for readers' advisory are available via paid subscription. These resources provide comprehensive lists of books with reviews and recommendations for similar titles, as well as other helpful information. A new database, *Reader's Advisor Online,* is produced by Libraries Unlimited, and subscription costs are based on the population that the library serves. Information for subscribing or obtaining a free trial can be found at http://rainfo.lu.com/ordering.aspx.

NoveList and *NoveList K-12* for children and teens comprise two other subscription databases that are available for readers' advisory. These databases are produced by EBSCO Publishing, and they feature over 147,000 fiction titles. Contact information and a free trial are available at http://www.epnet.com/thisTopic.php?topicID=16&marketID=6.

Vendor Web Sites

Although vendor Web sites do not provide specific readers' advisory services and resources like those provided by the subscription databases mentioned above, they can be used to find the titles of specific books on various topics, pricing information, and reviews of books. Some helpful vendor Web sites include the following:

- Baker & Taylor, Inc.: http://www.btol.com/
- Follett Library Resources' Titlewave: http://www.flr.follett.com/index.html
- Ingram Book Group: http://www.ingrambook.com/start/default.asp
- Mackin: http://www.mackin.com/

WEB RESOURCES

Libraries Unlimited's Genreflecting.com: http://www.genreflecting.com/—based on the highly respected Genreflecting readers' advisory book series, this site provides generous lists of books in various genres, definitions of genres, an interactive "Ask the Experts" section in which questions can be submitted to experts on various genres, and much more! This outstanding free resource is an invaluable tool for those who want to learn more about genre fiction.

Readers' Club: http://www.readersclub.org/default.asp—a site that provides a free e-mail newsletter, podcasts about books and authors, featured book lists, reviews of fiction, nonfiction, graphic novels, and novellas, and a "Teen Corner" with reviews of books in many genres of fiction—a great link to add to your teen library's Web site.

CHAPTER 5

Programming for Teens

WHAT IS LIBRARY PROGRAMMING?

Library programming simply means that the library plans and implements a variety of types of programs for a variety of reasons. Teen programming requires that the public library offer to its teen customers programs of interest to them rather than programs that parents or staff members necessarily deem "appropriate" or beneficial. While some programs for teens may indeed fit these descriptors, the most critical factor of any program that the library sponsors for teens is that it must be teen appealing. Otherwise, the programs are doomed to fail and cost the library money, time, and other resources, as well as sending a message to teens that the library's programs are "lame" or, at best, not very interesting. Thus, just as you seek input from your teen advisory board in other areas, do the same when planning programs. Programs can take many forms, several of which will be described later. Generally speaking, library programs can be of two types, entertainment or educational. Within these broad categories are literally hundreds of options, ranging from free, easy-to-implement programs to very expensive, complex programs, with lots of program ideas in between those extremes.

WHY DO IT? PURPOSES OF PROGRAMS

Some people say that library programming will greatly boost library use among attendees, and others say that it has little effect on library use. So if your sole reason for sponsoring programs is to increase your circulation or ensure that your teen library is full to running over with teenagers, don't do it! If, on the other hand, you believe that part of the public library's mission is to provide quality information, recreation, entertainment, and educational opportunities to folks in your community and to create a "sense of place" for all citizens, then library programming is a powerful tool for accomplishing that mission. If your library does experience heavier use as a result of the programs that are offered, consider it a bonus! Basically, if the public library is to effectively serve the common good, then part of the library's mission should address the provision of quality programs to all of your library's customers.

WHERE TO BEGIN

An excellent way to start the process of planning programs for teens is, you guessed it, ask them what they want and need. Although some of their ideas may be a bit lofty, with some guidance and clear parameters from which to proceed, teens will generate program ideas that are both doable and fun for them. You can generate ideas in one of several ways:

- Using some Web-based survey software such as *Survey Monkey*™, create an interactive survey on your Web site to gather input on teen programs.
- Have a short, hard-copy questionnaire at the circulation desk, and when teens check out materials, ask them to complete the questionnaire.
- Talk to teens informally to get their input and ideas for programs. This should be done on an ongoing basis.
- Place a program suggestion box somewhere visible in the teen area. Be sure to place slips of paper and a pen or pencil nearby.
- Ask teachers and other youth workers for program needs they have observed, based on their work with teens.
- Select some teens to participate in a focus group to brainstorm ideas for programs.
- Create a teen program task force whose job it is to generate program ideas and then help facilitate them.
- Using the library's patron database, contact teen customers by phone to get their input. Be sure to keep the call short, asking only two or three questions at most.
- At the end of a program, distribute a short evaluation form that includes a place for teens to make suggestions for future programs.

If you decide to convene a teen focus group to brainstorm ideas, be sure to invite some of your teen advisory board members to participate, as this group obviously has a vested interest in what is happening at the library. You can approach the focus group brainstorming session in one of two ways:

1. Simply let the group engage in an open brainstorming session in which there are no restrictions.
2. Clarify the guidelines to which the group must adhere, so that most if not all of the ideas generated are actually doable and will be taken under consideration.

If you use the first approach, it is critical that there are "no stupid ideas" and no value judgments aimed at anyone's ideas. Otherwise, individuals will shut down, and you will receive little input from that point on in the process. All ideas are initially accepted, and the process of narrowing and refining the list of ideas to those that are actually doable will be completed at a later time. The library's teen advisory board or teen program task force, or a combination of members of both groups, can do the refining process.

If you decide upon the second approach to brainstorming, then you will need to set some parameters for the group, in which you address such items as budget, time restraints, scheduling considerations, available space, and other areas within which you need to work. If an idea that is generated is not practical, go ahead and add it to the list. Then, during the second step in this process, ask the group to prioritize their list of ideas and narrow it to the number of programs you feel are reasonable within a certain time period, such as one year. Be sure to reward the teens for their time and assistance. Pizza works wonders!

A good way to start either type of session is to ask some questions to get teens to think about things that are important and enjoyable to them, such as their hobbies, reading interests and favorite authors, ways they spend their free time, favorite movies, and other topics as indicated in the following list of questions. Have someone write the answers on a flip chart or on white butcher paper. Then, after the group has started thinking about what they want or need, you can begin to conduct the brainstorming session to create a list of program ideas. Some questions to jump start the thinking process include the following:

- What do you like to do in your free time?
- Where do you like to hang out after school?
- What are your hobbies?
- If you had only one hour of free time, what would you like to do?
- What are some things you would you like to learn more about?
- What do you and your friends like to do together?
- What are your favorite books?
- What are your favorite movies?
- Who is your favorite local celebrity?
- Who is your favorite musician?
- Who is your favorite author?

- What kind of snacks do you like? (always a popular question!)
- What famous person in history would you like to know more about?
- What famous person of today would you like to know more about?
- What kinds of things do you like to create with your hands?
- What is your favorite type of music?
- What is your favorite sport?
- What kind of computer-based activities do you like?
- What kinds of computer or video games do you like to play?
- What do you and your friends like to talk about or think about?
- What is your favorite subject in school?

Remember that the questions are not program ideas at this point, but they will help the group generate ideas for programs when the actual brainstorming session starts.

Once the answers to the questions are written down, be sure to tape the sheets to the walls so that they will remain visible throughout the brainstorming session. Also, be sure to let the participants know what the next steps will be once the program ideas are developed. Do not promise them that all of the ideas will be put into practice, but instead, make it clear that these ideas are a starting place from which they and the staff will work to begin selecting and planning the programs that will actually be offered. However, it is imperative that at least some of the program ideas be implemented. Otherwise teen customers will feel that this exercise was meaningless and a waste of time. Once the program ideas are captured, the library staff's work begins.

ONCE I HAVE AN IDEA, WHAT NEXT?

Many excellent resources for program planning are available, and some of them are included in the bibliography of this book. A helpful way to approach the planning process is to ask the standard questions of "Who?" "What?" "When?" "Where?" "How?" "How much?" and "Why?" for each program that you are considering. The answers to these questions will give you a broad outline from which to work. Create a planning form using the information generated from these questions. Templates for a variety of forms to use for programming are available in Patrick Jones's 1992 book, *Connecting Young Adults and Libraries: A How-To-Do-It Manual.* Make sure to get the necessary approval from your supervisor or library board before moving into the actual planning process. However, it is helpful to have a preliminary plan to show your supervisor or board so that they will understand the purpose and the amount of support, especially financial support, needed for the proposed programs.

Once you have identified the answers to the standard questions and developed a planning form, then you can begin the actual planning process. Basic steps for the process are given below. These can, of course, be modified to meet the specific needs of your library.

Develop a firm budget for the program. Your preliminary planning document should include an estimated cost, but you will need to refine the estimate so that it will accurately reflect all the costs associated with the program.

Check and double check to make sure that you have everything needed to deliver the program. This includes items such as adequate space, technology, materials of all kinds, extra staff, parent chaperones if necessary, the presenter or speaker (booked), refreshments, and all other items that you have listed on your planning form.

Promote your program. There are many ways in which this can be done, such as ads on your Web site; press releases to local media; ads in the local newspaper, radio station, or TV station; announcements on the PA system at the local high schools; announcements to various parent groups in the community; announcements to various teen groups in the community; fliers on students' car windshields at the high schools (check first to be sure this is permitted); ads posted on school cafeteria bulletin boards and other bulletin boards throughout the school; ads on bulletin boards in local churches; fliers distributed by teachers at the high schools; and fliers distributed by various school clubs and committees to their members.

Invite teen customers. Although your programs will probably be open to all teens in the community, if you have space limitations, you may want to issue free tickets on a first-come, first-served basis so that you can adequately accommodate all who want to attend. Make it a point to personally invite those teen customers who frequent the library, and post an invitation on the teen pages of your Web site to reach a broader audience. Although this may seem redundant in light of the fact that you will be promoting the program via fliers that will be available throughout the community, an actual invitation sends a message to teens that you truly care about them as individuals.

With regard to issuing tickets, although you should not charge a fee to attend a library program, you might want to consider asking for a donation such as a canned food item to be given to a local social services agency. This strategy sends two messages: (1) the library's programs are worth the cost of a contribution; and (2) the library is a contributing member of the community that seeks to help those who are in need. Another way to motivate teens to attend programs is to waive library fines for those who come to the library to get their program tickets on a designated day.

Make sure that all logistical details are planned for well in advance of each program. Nothing will kill a program faster than a dead microphone or sound system, a PowerPoint™ crash, a frigidly cold room, or a myriad of other details. Have the attitude that "whatever can go wrong, will go wrong," and have a contingency plan for every facet of your program.

Make sure to have plenty of adults and teens scheduled to help with the program. Adult helpers can be staff members, parents, community members, or a combination of these. Teen advisory board members or program task force members can be enlisted to help as well. This is yet another way to get teens involved.

Present the program! When the big day arrives, do a final check on everything that is needed, and be prepared with a "Plan B" in case anything goes wrong. For example, if a speaker has a PowerPoint™ slide show planned, save a backup copy of the show on a flash drive, and have both the flash drive and a backup computer available in case something happens to the primary computer. Make arrangements to borrow a portable sound system in case the library's system stops working.

In a worst-case scenario such as a devastating storm that closes airports and prevents your speaker from arriving, always have a backup plan in mind, for example, asking a local celebrity to be "on call" to fill in, offering some kind of hands-on art or craft activity, or having a variety of board and computers games available to change the focus to a gaming event if necessary.

Evaluate the program. Immediately after the program, be ready to distribute a *short* and easy-to-complete evaluation form to all attendees. If possible, give attendees some type of incentive to complete and turn in the forms. Inexpensive items such as jazzy-looking pens or pencils, a lanyard to hold a flash drive, an autographed photo of the speaker, or bookmarks with access to a passworded Web site on which teens can get more information about the topic or speaker will provide motivation to teens to complete and submit their evaluations.

After the program evaluations have been submitted, it is imperative that library staff and teens that helped with the program review the evaluations and use them when planning future programs. In fact, program evaluations can be used later on when you start the brainstorming session for the next round of programs.

As far as is possible, use a numerical rating system in which participants simply circle a number from 1 to 5 or 1 to 3, with 1 being the lowest rating and 3 or 5, depending upon the range, being the highest. At the end of the evaluation form, you will want to include a few questions that probe for additional, important information, questions such as, "How did you find out about this program?" "What other types of programs would you like the library to sponsor?" and "What could have been done to make this program better?" Some sample questions to ask on the program evaluation form, using a scale of 1 to 5 approach, are as follows:

- What overall rating would you give this program?
- Was the program scheduled at a convenient time?
- How interesting was the topic of this program?
- How well did the speaker do in presenting this program?
- How would you compare this presentation to other presentations you have heard on this topic?
- What are the chances that you would attend a program like this in the future?
- How likely are you to recommend that your friends attend a program at the library?
- How likely are you to attend another program given at the library?

In addition to asking participants to evaluate the program, you should also conduct an internal evaluation. You will want to examine those things that went well, as well as those items that need to be changed in the next program. The questions included on this evaluation will require more in-depth answers to help guide the planning process for the next round of programs. Questions could include the following:

- How well was the planning process conducted?
- What needed to be changed or added to the planning process?
- Did you have adequate help from library staff and other adults?
- Did this topic meet the needs or desires of the teens who attended?
- Was the attendance adequate?
- Was the program scheduled at a convenient time for teens?
- Were the promotional activities effective? If not, what needed to be done differently?
- Did you effectively use teens' input when planning the program?
- Did you involve teens throughout the process?
- What went well on the day of the program?
- What did not go well on the day of the program?
- Was this program worthy of the time, money, and other effort spent?
- Would you offer a program like this again? Why? Why not?

Create and maintain a file of all documents used for programs. Literally every piece of paper or electronic document that you created and used to plan and evaluate a program should be kept in a file for future use. These could be invaluable for planning future programs. Note: it is important that you review the files from time to time and get rid of them when they are no longer useful.

TYPES OF PROGRAMS

As previously mentioned, library programs fall into one of two broad categories: educational or entertainment. Within those two categories are many, many subcategories, such as recreational, informational, special interest, cultural, active or passive programs, group or individually focused programs, ongoing or one-time programs, and many others. Within the subcategories are also many specific types of programs, some of which are presented below. When you begin to plan programs, remember that it is not the type of program that is important but rather whether the programs offered meet the needs and desires of your teen customers. Thus, you may find that all of your programs are of one particular type, and this is perfectly fine, as long as the programs continue to be well attended and received. Let your teen customers drive the focus of your programs as far as possible, but be ready to change directions and focus when you see that something new is needed. This means, of course, that you need to continue to solicit input from teens on an ongoing basis about the types of programs they would like the library to offer.

The program suggestions that follow are listed in no particular order; again, before you decide which ones to implement, you will need to get input from your teen customers.

BOOK CLUBS

The traditional book club is one in which the members of a group of teens all read the same book and then get together to discuss it. Sometimes either a teen leader or an adult staff member will prepare questions to discuss, and sometimes the discussion is more free form, with no particular focus. As with all types of book clubs, the most critical factor is book selection. If a book of high interest to teen participants is selected, the book club can be a lively, vital type of program. If, on the other hand, the book that is selected is not appealing, a book club will quickly die. Therefore, it is imperative that the library staff facilitating the book club be knowledgeable about literature that teens will like, know the interests and reading tastes of the teens that are attending the book club, and solicit teens' input when selecting a book to read. One other note about book selection: Patrick Jones suggests that when recommending books to teens you should make sure that the book is not below a teen's reading ability or age group level (1992, 86). Not only is this critical when providing readers' advisory services, but it also holds true when selecting books for book clubs. Teens will be turned off if a book selected appears to be too easy for them or if it addresses topics that are of interest to younger children.

While the traditional approach may be very effective, you may find that this type of book club is not appealing to the teens with whom you work. If this is the case, then you may want to think about modifying the structure to better meet the needs of your library's teen customers. Given below are some variations on book clubs that you may want to consider. Be sure to solicit input from your teen advisory board before you decide upon the approach(es) that will be best suited to your teen customers.

Guys Only Book Club or Girls Only Book Club: The advantage of this type of book club is that you can select and read literature that is highly appealing to the participating gender. Guys may like books in the adventure genre, while girls may prefer chick lit, for example. Girls may prefer books that feature a female protagonist, while guys may want to read about a male protagonist. Questions and follow-up activities could be designed to be more specific in nature so that they are more relevant to the participants.

Online "Book" Club: This type of book club could be structured in many ways. You could post on the teen Web site a specific book title and assign sections of the book to be read each month or week. Then, you could create a wiki in which participants could enter their comments or answers to discussion questions. Another approach could be to structure this book club around the content of a particular educational or recreational Web site. Questions would be posed about the information on the Web site, and participants could respond via the wiki. Members of the book club could suggest other Web sites for the group to access and discuss.

For a totally different approach, rather than using textual material for the club to read, you could find video clips for participants to view and discuss. In this case, you might want to give the club a name that better reflects the structure, such as the *Virtual Viewing Club* or something similar but with a catchier title. Caution: make sure that you are very familiar with the sites and content that will be used, so that they are appropriate for your group.

The Non-Book Book Club: The reading focus of this group could be teen magazines rather than books. This type of club could be highly appealing to reluctant or struggling readers, due to the limited amount of text included in the reading material that is selected. To make this club even more appealing, some of the discussions could center on graphical material, such as photos, rather than textual material. Other types of material that this group could use are newspapers, newsletters, such as their school newsletter, travel brochures or other literature provided by the local chamber of commerce, how to do it–type manuals or handbooks that provide information on topics such as skateboarding or computer gaming, and any number of other types of material that have limited amounts of text and useful or attractive photos or diagrams.

Graphic Novel Club: This book club could be narrowed down by specific type of graphic novel such as a *Manga Club* or an *Anime Club,* for example. The books selected would, of course, fit into the specific type of graphic novel around which the group is organized. In addition to reading the graphic novels, participants may want to dress in the style of their favorite characters and actually read sections of the books aloud during meetings.

Sci Fi (or other genre) Book Club: Since this type of genre-based book club is limited in focus, it may also be limited in attendance. However, because teens are so peer dependent, it is possible that there are large numbers of teens in your community that enjoy reading in a particular genre. Ask high school English teachers or school librarians if this is the case among the students with whom they work. If so, you have an excellent opportunity to develop a strong group of teen library supporters using this approach.

Contemporary Literature Book Club: Sometimes publishers will send advance reading copies of books or unproofed galleys to librarians if they will agree to have teens read these books and provide written book reviews. For teens who like to read and write, this type of club is very appealing. Send a query letter to publishers to find out whether they are willing to send copies for teens to read. Not only will teens enjoy the fact that they are the first group to read these brand-new books, but they will also be pleased to know that the publishers are relying on them for input.

Teen and Parent Book Club: While this may not seem an appropriate type of book club to be included in a book about teen library services, it can indeed be a powerful tool for gaining support and participation from the parents of your teen customers. This group would read teen novels or adult novels popular with teens and then discuss them in a traditional book club process. The goal would not be to create readers of teen books among participants but rather to expose parents to the types of teen books that are available and help them become aware of some of the issues included in these books.

Since some of the books written for teens and some of the adult books that teens like contain graphic material (in the sense of including sexual content and violence), this club could also provide a way for parents to better understand and accept these materials rather than stumbling upon some of the books their child is reading and being shocked at the content. Although the purpose of the group would not be the prevention of book challenges, this could well be a side benefit. As parents become more knowledgeable about what teens are reading, they will have opportunities to engage in dialogue with their teens about sensitive issues and their family's values.

A SAMPLING OF PROGRAMS

Entertainment and educational programs are as numerous as they are varied in appeal. To decide on which type of entertainment or educational programs your library should offer, you absolutely MUST get input from your teen customers. What is popular in one community may fall flat in another. For example, if you live in a mountainous or desert area, offering a program on scuba diving may not be practical. On the other hand, if your town is near an ocean, such a program may be in high demand. Programs below vary greatly, so you and your teen advisory board will need to determine the needs in your local community when you select from lists of programs. Note that the types of programs discussed below have rather generic titles. You and your teen advisory board may want to jazz these up to make the themes or titles more appealing and engaging. In addition to the sample program types given below, many public libraries have program listings available on the Web from which you can gain ideas. Some of these Web sites are listed in the Web Resources section at the end of this chapter to further assist you in developing your programs.

Teen Writers' Contest: This type of program can be a follow-up to a *Teen Writer's Workshop* that will be delivered to interested teens to help them get started on writing a short story, poem, or other item that they will enter in the contest. Specific rules for your contest will vary as you determine exactly what parameters will work with your teen customers. Be sure that the contest is widely advertised and that you submit a follow-up article to all of the local media, in which you list the participants and winners.

Create Your Own Teen Novel: Authors David Lubar and Dian Curtis Regan have created a Web page (www.davidlubar.com/yakit.html) providing a framework for a plot that can be adapted and used as a starting place from which teens can write a novel. Note that the creators of the Web site are children's book authors, so you will want to revise the plot to be more appropriate for teens, but this Web site can give you ideas for "story starters" that would work. The story outline provides a fill in the blank–type approach to jump start the thinking process for writing a teen novel.

Book Check Out Contest: This program is simple to administer and low cost. All teen customers have to do is check out a book, and their names will be entered into a drawing for some type of prize. The more times teens check out books, the more times their names are entered into the prize drawing. Prizes could be as simple as a Christmas ornament or something a bit more library related, such as a paperback copy of a new teen novel.

Duct Tape Doins: A just for fun activity for teens that will result in lots of laughter, this program is a one-time event in which teens create items using standard duct tape. Teens can make items such as jewelry, purses, wallets, clothing, shoes, and flowers. While this program may have no educational value, it can be a wacky way to attract teens to the library, and is obviously a low-cost event.

Spot the Fake Contest: Teens love to "out" things and ideas that are false. This contest could be developed around one of many themes, such as fake Web sites, fake animals, fake authors and book titles, fake events or people in local history, fake names of towns in the state, and many others. This program is another one that will be quick, easy, and inexpensive. Prizes can be awarded for correct answers in one or more categories. An excellent follow-up program would be one that is focused on one of the categories in the contest. For example, a local historian could present a program elaborating on what "really happened" in a specific event in history, for example, rather than the "fakes" upon which the contest was based.

Design a Poster Contest: Teens would create a poster (or flyer, or brochure, or greeting card) that could be used to announce a special holiday, event, library program, community celebration, or an art object of some kind to decorate the library. As with the other contests, some type of prize could be awarded for the top entries, or, alternatively, all participants could be rewarded with special checkout privileges, additional access to computer games, a party at which the artwork is displayed, or simply by having their names included in an article in the local newspaper.

Write a Song Contest: This is similar to the contest above, but would involve writing a piece of music. The winners could be rewarded by being given the opportunity to perform their music at a special event, or, alternatively, all the participants could perform their pieces. Enlist a local music teacher to help plan and judge this contest.

Gaming Night or Gaming Club: If you are not well versed in planning and hosting computer-based gaming events, rely on teens who are expert gamers to help you. You may need to ask your teen library advisory board members to refer you to teens who have expertise in this area. This type of program may have a limited appeal, but one important benefit would be attracting teens who do not typically use the library, and therefore increasing your teen customer base.

Dance Dance Revolution™ (DDR) Night: As with a computer gaming program, you may need assistance from teens who are DDR fans in planning this type of program. DDR is a particular type of computer/video-based game that requires participants to "dance" or move their feet to music according to the graphical patterns that appear on the video screen. If there is a video arcade in your town or nearby, visit it to see DDR participants in action. The software and accompanying equipment can be quite expensive. However, it may well be that teens in your community would be willing to let the library borrow these items for use in a program.

Teen Library Friends Group: Some of the programs listed above may be one-time events, but a friends group can be ongoing. Meeting schedules, topics presented, projects, and all other aspects of this group will be customized based on input from participants with the guidance of library staff. As with an adult friends group, one purpose could be fund-raising, but many other activities are possible. The primary purpose of the group would be for members to support the library and to act as library ambassadors among their peers.

Teen Movie Night: Think out of the box on this one, as you will need to be sure that the movies you are showing can be legally shown to groups of teens. Some movie producers and distributors provide public performance rights, and fees for these rights vary greatly. Thus, you may not be able to show first-run, popular movies but might instead find some B movies or documentaries on topics of interest to teens. See the Web site created by Dr. Carol Simpson, included in the Web Resources section at the end of this chapter, for a list of producers that provide public performance rights.

Online Teen Library Zine: Teens who like to write are great candidates for producing and maintaining an electronic magazine to be made available to all teens in the community. The magazine can include articles of interest to teens, book and movie reviews, editorials and commentaries by teens, regular columns on topics of interest to teens, and informational items such as announcements of upcoming library events. Make sure to get written permission from parents before including any photographs of teens in the magazine.

Teen Reading/Library Partners: This program involves recruiting teens to read with and to younger children, either as a part of a summer reading program or as an ongoing project. In addition to reading to children, teens could also present programs to children, give puppet shows, volunteer to work in the children's library, help select children's books to add to the collection, and teach children how to use the online catalog or other computer programs.

Peer Readers' Advisory Club: Just as the name implies, this program would involve teens who are willing to read books and reviews and make recommendations to their peers about good books. The selections could be included in an electronic magazine as a regular column, provided as an annotated list on the teen Web page, or included in a special teen readers' advisory blog. Another method of distributing lists of books produced by this group would be to create an e-mail distribution list. Of course, from time to time, this group could also host meetings at which they would give book talks to their peers and present the books they are recommending.

Media Discussion Group: Rather than reading and discussing books, this group would meet to discuss movies, TV shows, documentary videos, computer games, or music. Each meeting could have a theme, such as the top 10 video rentals for the month as included in some nationally published newspaper or magazine; the top 10 music albums; specific topics, such as politics or the environment, that are addressed in well-known documentaries; teen issues and characters in movies or TV shows; concerts on the public television station; and others.

Serial Novels (or Graphic Novels) on the Web Program: Teens who like to write or illustrate would meet regularly to create their own teen novel or graphic novel that would be published in serial format on the library's teen Web page. The serial works would need to be reviewed and possibly edited by a library staff member or other adult volunteer. This program could be planned to produce just one novel, or it could be an ongoing program in which the participants vary from novel to novel.

Food and Fiction: Like the "dinner and a movie" concept, this program involves a fiction book discussion accompanied by the generous provision of food and beverages for teens. The food is as important as the book discussion, so do not scrimp on the cuisine. The food can consist of an entire meal, lots of appetizers and beverages, or desserts. Consider a theme for the food that goes along with the book. The food can either be purchased or prepared and contributed by the participants. Be sure to let participants know about ingredients such as peanuts or other items to which some people may be allergic.

Career Nights: Some schools host career days on which they invite community members from various professions to give presentations about the experience and educational background necessary for their careers. Check with the high schools in your community to find out whether career days are planned. If they are, consider partnering with the schools to extend the program by offering follow-up activities and informational resources for teens. If the schools in your community do not provide career days, then the library can provide a series of presentations on various careers. Your online teen magazine could feature a series of articles on various careers as presentations on specific careers are given at the library.

Digital Photography for Teens: This program would consist of a series of classes on using digital cameras, editing photos, posting photos on various Web sites, choosing printers to use, and many other topics related to digital photography. If the program proves popular, your library could offer an advanced series in which more complex techniques are presented.

Teen Art Club: An art club could be an ongoing program, or it could be scheduled for a designated period of time, at the end of which each participant would have a piece of artwork for display. The program could be geared toward one particular type of art, such as watercolor painting, sculpture, or work in some other medium, and a local artist could be enlisted to teach teens how to paint or create in that medium. Another approach would be a craft club in which one particular type of craft would be taught, such that each participant would have a product at the end of the scheduled classes. The variations on this particular program are limited only by the artistic expertise in your community.

Wikis, Podcasts, and Blogs, Oh My!: This program would cover new and emerging technologies. Thus, it would be continually evolving as new technologies become available. Participants would learn how to use the technologies and apply them to various projects for homework assignments or personal use. If social networking sites are included, make sure to follow Internet safety precautions, and obtain parental permission before allowing participants to set up their own pages on sites such as *MySpace*™ or *Facebook*.™

Teen Outdoor Enthusiasts: Participants would learn about outdoor activities such as camping, hiking, biking, skiing, snowboarding, in-line skating, canoeing, rafting, swimming, and others, depending upon the opportunities available in your community. The program could be held in the library or it could be held outside to allow participants to actually engage in an activity. If specific equipment would be required, it would be necessary to let participants know what to bring or wear prior to the first session. To highlight the resources available at the library, some light "research" could be done during the first session, in which participants would use the library's databases, magazines, books, and other items in the collection to learn about the activities involved.

The Sports Arena: This program could be structured in a variety of ways. Participants could actually view live or recorded sporting events on television and then discuss them. Local athletes could serve as speakers and give presentations on their sport. Participants could read about various sports in books or magazines or on Web sites and then discuss them. Documentaries on the rules of certain sports or how to play them could be shown. Computer or video games involving various sports could be used.

Origami for Teens: As with the other art- or craft-oriented programs, this one would provide participants with a hands-on opportunity to create origami objects that could be displayed in the library and then kept for personal use. Participants could also teach younger children simple origami in conjunction with the summer reading program.

Spinning a Tale: A Storyteller's Workshop for Teens: Stories are appealing for all ages, and teens are no exception. A local storyteller could present techniques for storytelling and teach teens several stories that they could tell to different audiences. If no local storyteller is available, library staff could use storytelling books and DVDs to teach teens how to be effective storytellers. As with the origami program and some others, teens could practice their skills, in this case by telling stories to younger children, as part of the summer reading program or another program.

Cool Crafts for Teens: The operative word here is "cool." The craft items to be produced need to appeal to teenagers. A good approach is to bring several examples to the first session and let participants decide what they would like to make. Consider such items as cell phone cases, fancy lanyards for flash drives, MP3 cases and other tech-type objects, along with more traditional items such as billfolds, purses, jewelry, and checkbook covers.

Cooking Club: For this program to be effective and interesting, it, like other programs in which things are made or created, should be hands on. Thus, unless the library has a full-service kitchen, another location may be necessary. The focus of a cooking club could be general in nature or address only one type of food, such as desserts. To keep costs down, you could solicit donations of ingredients from local grocery stores. Sometimes items are still usable, even though their expiration dates have passed. Stores are sometimes required to discard these items but may be willing to donate some of them to the library for this program. Make sure to ask the store manager whether the items are still safe to be eaten.

Animal Lovers Club: The content and format of this program are limited only by your imagination. The program could include lectures and demonstrations by local veterinarians, visits to the local humane society, presentations by staff from a local zoo, lessons by a local trainer on how to train a dog, or many other presentations. The program could also provide participants with opportunities to read and discuss books about animals, either fiction or nonfiction.

Evening with an Author: This program is typically a one-time event, or is held only once a year due to cost. If you have local authors who are willing either to volunteer their time or to charge only a small fee, this program may be presented at little cost. If you decide to bring in a nationally known author, obviously the costs will be higher and will include not only a speaker's fee but travel costs. However, if an author is well known to teenagers and is a good presenter, the expense may be well worth it. Do your homework before inviting an author to speak. Some excellent writers are not competent speakers. Before you contract with an author or agent, ask for referrals, and check references to find out how well the author relates to teen audiences. One other note: solicit input from your teen advisory board on authors they would like to hear, rather than making this decision on your own. Many authors make their contact information available on their Web sites, and some can be contacted via e-mail rather than by long-distance phone calls.

Beauty from the Inside Out: This program would be for teen girls, and it would include information on good manners, character, social skills, and, of course, beauty tips for hair, dress, and makeup. Although this program could be in the form of a one-time workshop, it could also be delivered in a series of classes in which experts in each area would present information and then give participants time to try out some of the ideas presented. If participants would be required to bring specific items to sessions, librarians should be sure to specify this in the program description.

EVENTS-BASED PROGRAMS

Programs in this category are developed to coincide with or support a particular holiday, celebration, event, season, or other specific situation. Like other programs, they may consist of one-time events or series of presentations or activities. Many of the programs in Amy Alessio and Kimberly Patton's book *A Year of Programs for Teens* (2007) fall into this category. They include programs for each month of the year, varying from programs that are very easy and inexpensive to implement to others that are more complex and costly, and complete information is provided for planning and delivering each program. Thus, this book is a useful resource for those who may be planning teen programs for the first time.

Another helpful resource for planning events-based programs for teens is the YALSA Web site. It includes a listing of yearly special events, such as Teen Tech Week, as well as resources that can be purchased from the ALA Online Store to help promote the programs. In addition to lists of events, the YALSA Web site also features information on authors and many lists of award-winning books for teens that could be selected for teen book clubs.

Examples of some events and holidays upon which programs can be based are given below. Some are sponsored or celebrated by specific organizations such as YALSA, and others are nationally recognized celebrations. Most well-known holidays are not included.

- January

    - Presidents' Day
    - National Hobby Month
    - National Oatmeal Month

- February

    - Black History Month
    - Chinese New Year
    - Library Lovers Month
    - Super Bowl Sunday

- March

    - Teen Tech Week
    - Read Across America
    - Music in Our Schools Month
    - Women in History Month
    - National Education Week

- April

    - National Library Week
    - Teen Literature Day
    - Poetry Month
    - Young People's Poetry Week
    - School Library Media Month
    - TV Turn Off Week
    - Earth Day

- May

    - Get Caught Reading Month
    - National Hamburger Month

- June

    - Candy Month
    - Adopt a Cat Month
    - Flag Day

- July
  - Hammock Day
  - National Hotdog Month
  - National Ice Cream Month

- August
  - Family Fun Month
  - National Picnic Month

- September
  - Library Card Sign Up Month
  - Banned Books Week
  - Constitution Day

- October
  - Teen Read Week
  - Teens' Top Ten Voting
  - Make a Difference Day

- November
  - Family Literacy Day
  - Peanut Butter Lover's Month
  - Aviation History Month

- December
  - Human Rights Day
  - Bill of Rights Day
  - Boxing Day

Additional interesting and unusual holidays and celebrations can be found at the Holiday Insights Web site. The URL is listed in the Web Resources section at the end of this chapter. Use the list provided, add others to consider as program tie-ins, and create an annual schedule of holidays, celebrations, and events that you can use over and over again. Be sure to update the list from time to time as you learn about new events and celebrations that you want to add.

SUMMER READING PROGRAMS

Since many of the children who are your library customers are familiar with the annual children's summer reading program, it can be easy to "sell" a teen summer reading program, provided that participants in the children's program had a positive experience. Therefore, make sure to ask these young customers and their parents to help you evaluate the children's summer reading program, and consider their input when planning your teen program. Keep in mind that you will need to ratchet up the activities and incentives so that they are appropriate for teens. Otherwise, the program may be viewed by your teen customers as simply a modified children's program, and that will be the kiss of death!

How Does the Program Work?

As with other types of programs, the teen summer reading program can be as distinctive as you like, but the basic structure of the teen program, like the children's program, is that teens will read books, magazines, graphic novels, or other print or online material; fill out some type of form verifying what they have read; and either submit a specific number of required forms in order to earn a prize or put forms into a container each week to be entered into a drawing for a prize. The details can vary greatly, depending upon your budget, the number of library staff members available to help with the program, the number of teens enrolled, and the length of the program. Most programs start some time in June and finish at the end of July so that they are completed by the time school starts.

If a teen summer reading program is sponsored by your state library, you can adopt the annual theme and program ideas provided by this organization. Simply go to your state library's Web site or contact the state library by phone to find out about the theme and obtain program ideas and promotional items. The state library typically develops high-quality promotional items and public relations (PR) pieces to advertise the program, so that much of the preplanning has already been done for you. If you have not previously organized a teen summer reading program, using the state's program might be the easiest way to start.

Planning Tips

If you choose to present an original teen summer reading program, you will want to begin the planning process well in advance of the starting date. You will need to engage in such planning activities as meeting with the teen library advisory board to solicit input and ideas, preparing PR pieces such as fliers and posters, advertising the program in the local media, developing activities and project ideas, preparing materials, ordering books and other reading items, purchasing incentives, enrolling participants, organizing library staff, decorating the teen area with posters and other items to announce the program, visiting schools to give presentations about it, putting PR pieces in places that teens frequent, such as clubs and churches, and developing a calendar of events.

Make sure that there is money in your budget to support the program. Do not scrimp on funds for items such as popular new fiction books, materials for the program, and incentives to make it a success. Otherwise, word will quickly spread that the program is not worthwhile, and your teen customers will find other activities to occupy their time during the summer.

A Word about Incentives

Although you do not need to spend exorbitant amounts of money for incentives, you do need to make sure that the incentives are items that are popular with teens. Again, ask your teen advisory board for suggestions and ideas. Something as simple as extra computer/Internet time or special access to new books, graphic novels, or magazines may be attractive to your teen customers. On the other hand, you may want to purchase at least one expensive grand prize to be awarded at the end of the program. Solicit donations from local businesses or philanthropic organizations, as they often need to make tax deductible charitable donations. Consider having various levels of incentives based on the number of items read or the number of minutes spent reading. Prizes can be graduated according to increased numbers of items or minutes. Make sure that you have ample reading items for those teens that are reluctant or struggling readers, so that they can be successful in earning incentives.

Some Dos and Don'ts

- Do make the program fun! While this may seem self-evident, reading can be laborious for some teens, so find ways to get them reading that do not feel like homework assignments. Examples: reading cereal boxes, labels on video games, teen blogs or wikis, and other unusual items.
- Do provide generous numbers of incentives. Again, these can be graduated in value, but everyone should be able to earn at least a few incentives during the program.
- Do provide a wide variety of types and levels of reading material.
- Do allow teens to print out reading material such as blogs and wikis so that they can read lengthier items at home.
- Do allow teens to check out magazines if they do not have time or space to read them in the library.
- Do involve parents in the program in a way that is supportive but not obtrusive, so that teens do not feel they are being closely supervised.
- Do make the teen area comfortable so that teens can read in the library whenever possible.
- Do include varied weekly activities that are fun and engaging throughout the program.
- Don't create excessive rules or barriers that will stifle participation and interest.
- Don't repeat activities from previous summer programs.
- Don't expect all teen participants to like or participate in all of the activities. Individuals will attend the activities that they enjoy, and that's OK.

- Don't forget to have participants evaluate the program at the end. The information gained can be invaluable when you begin to plan next year's program.

SCHOOL VISITS

Public library staff members typically visit elementary schools to promote the children's summer reading program, but teens seldom see the public library staff except when visiting the library. I think this is a mistake. Public library staff should visit secondary schools throughout the year so that teens will see them, know who they are, and start to feel comfortable with them. However, given the enormous amount of content that most teachers must teach to meet state curriculum mandates, teachers may sometimes be reluctant to take time out for visits from outsiders. Thus, when you visit schools, it is important that you have a clear purpose for doing so and take as little time as possible out of the school day. Also, any presentations or announcements that you make must be relevant and interesting to teens. Otherwise, eyes will roll and sighs will abound when you walk through the classroom or school library doors.

Getting Your Foot in the Door

ALWAYS get permission from the principal or other school administrator before visiting a school! When you contact the person in charge, be sure to identify yourself, and clearly specify the purpose of the visit, the length of time you will need, and the classroom, library, or teacher you plan to visit in order to present your program or event. Then, after permission is granted, talk to the teacher or school librarian whom you will be visiting, to acquaint them with the purpose of your visit and other details. Take a minimal amount of time for your visit, and make sure to send a written thank you note to all concerned, as well as providing them with any other information you feel might be pertinent, such as the students' response to the program or event you have described to them. You should also send forms that you might want students to complete, tickets or other items that you would like the school staff to distribute, and personal invitations for the adults to the program or event.

Purposes of Visits

If a phone call or e-mail message will suffice to get your message across, then do not make a visit to a school. However, if your message will be more effective when delivered in person, then plan to visit the school instead. Sometimes all you might need to do is drop materials off in the office, but be sure to verify that the materials will be distributed, and include your contact information on the materials you drop off, so that students can follow up with questions if necessary. The reasons to visit a school may include the following:

- To announce a special speaker or a program that will be held at the library;
- To announce a special author presentation that will be held at the library;
- To distribute special tickets to limited-seating events. Before you visit, make sure you decide exactly who is eligible to receive the tickets;
- To give a short "preview" of a program or event via a video recording or PowerPoint show;
- To give a presentation about the summer reading program and distribute enrollment forms. If possible, have students complete the forms and turn them in to you before you leave;
- To explain the registration process for the teen summer reading program;
- To award special grand prizes to summer reading program winners;
- To talk with the librarian or classroom teachers about services, resources, and programs the public library can provide to them;
- To collaborate with the school librarian on special events or programs that you will offer jointly; and
- To give previews of new services, resources, and programs that the library is offering to students or teachers.

Partnering with schools can be a powerful method of promoting the public library's programs and services, as well as an excellent communication tool for working with educators to better meet the needs of teen customers, as well as educators' needs. Thus, it is a win/win option to work diligently to make this partnership successful.

WEB RESOURCES

Holiday Insights: http://holidayinsights.com—a site that includes multiple lists of holidays, celebrations, and other events, some of which are "bizarre and unique."

Imaginon: The Joe and Joan Martin Center's Teen Programs Page: http://www.library loft.org—this lists and describes programs for teens by topic.

The Public Library of Charlotte and Mecklenburg County's Programs and Events Listings: http://plcmc.org/Programs/programListing.asp—this lists programs and events by type, with age ranges and descriptions of all programs offered.

Public Performance Rights by Dr. Carol Simpson: http://courses.unt.edu/scimpson/cright/ppr.htm—a listing of producers and distributors of audiovisual media that grant public performance rights.

CHAPTER 6

Creating a Teen-Friendly Library

A HOME OF THEIR OWN: THE TEEN SPACE

Whether it's a cozy corner with a couple of bean bag chairs and some posters and potted plants or an entire high-tech center, complete with an outside commons area designated for young adults, your teen customers deserve to have a home of their own. Teens want and need to know that they have a space that is set aside just for them, a place where they can meet their friends, listen to music, work on their homework, cruise the Internet, or curl up with a good book. All too often, young adult or teen spaces are included in the children's section or the adult reference section, or worse yet, are nonexistent. Teens are special customers with their own wants and needs, and regardless of available space or budget constraints, it is usually possible to create a unique and inviting space to accommodate them, in a style and within an environment in which they will feel comfortable. Not only will having a teen space be beneficial to the library's teen customers, but it will also make other customers feel more comfortable, particularly parents of teens who are seeking a safe "third place" (besides home or school) for their teenage children.

In order to begin planning the teen library space, several factors will need to be considered, such as the purpose or function of the space, environment, location, arrangement or floor plan, furniture and equipment, and shelving and collection arrangement.

Just as a teen library advisory board can help address issues and develop policies and procedures that will govern your teen customers' use of the library in general, this group or a separate teen planning committee can also play an integral part in the planning, creation, and maintenance of the teen library space. As you read this chapter, think about how the teen library advisory board or planning committee can be utilized in helping to create a vital and viable teen center. The teen library customer's voice should resonate throughout the process of planning and setting up your teen library space.

PURPOSE AND FUNCTIONS

Before the planning process begins, library staff, with input from the teen planning committee, must thoroughly identify and define how the teen library space will be utilized. Questions to ask include the following: What is the purpose for this space? How will it be utilized? The staff and teen committee cannot answer these questions in a vacuum, but must instead review the overall mission and philosophy of the library, making sure that the teen space's purpose and uses are aligned with the mission and philosophy as a whole. Just as the library should have in place written philosophy and mission statements that undergird and drive the collection development and maintenance process, so should the library have a philosophy and mission statement that will help the staff and the teen library planning group decide on the purpose and functions of the teen library space.

Typically the library's philosophy and mission statements are written, board-approved documents. After thoroughly reviewing the overall mission and philosophy statements, staff and the teen planning group can begin to develop questions about how the facility will be used, questions that will, in turn, help with the planning process. Some considerations with regard to the uses/functions of the teen library space are listed below. This is not an exhaustive list, but it can provide a starting point from which additional ideas can flow. The potential functions for the teen library space may include the following:

- Social center and teen "hangout"
- Research and homework center
- Technology lab
- Information commons
- Gaming arcade, including computer and board games
- Area providing e-mail and chat services
- Viewing/listening area
- Free reading area
- Area for browsing and reading periodicals (magazines and newspapers)
- Meeting place for teen civic clubs
- Tutoring services area

- Computer training area
- Computer design studio (for computer-assisted designing, podcasts, video production, PowerPoint™ shows, etc.)
- Online learning lab (for distance education courses of personal interest)
- Arts and crafts area
- Meeting place for book discussion groups
- Paperback swap library
- Coffee shop or teen bistro
- School supplies store
- Meeting place for teen community or civic groups
- Family meeting place
- Area providing community "bulletin board" services—either electronic or physical

ENVIRONMENT

Obviously, the environment in the teen library should be teen friendly and comfortable for teens, but the area may also need to be a bit nontraditional in terms of typical thinking about what a library should look like. This means that library staff may need to abandon the standard library furnishings in favor of furniture and equipment more like those that teens have in their own favorite hangouts. In free reading and browsing areas, for example, the furniture should be comfortable and similar to the furniture that teens have in their own bedrooms, such as beanbag chairs or large throw pillows, and comfy, durable, and easy-to-move sofas and chairs. There should be good but nonobtrusive lighting; easy access to all types of material, from popular fiction and magazines to homework materials, music CDs, videos/DVDs, and computers, displayed face out as in bookstores; attractive displays; and collection arrangements that are engaging and easy to browse. Technology should be pervasive throughout the teen area so that teens can quickly move from one task to another without undue effort. Overall, the teen library space should convey a sense of privacy and comfort, as well as fostering both individual use and group interaction.

LOCATION

Teens should be able to see and easily access their area upon entering the library. This can be accomplished in one of several ways: (1) by providing a separate entrance to the teen library from the outside, making sure that this separate entrance is well supervised and safe; (2) by locating the teen area close to the main entrance of the library; or (3) by placing highly visible signage near the main entrance to direct teens to their space. Since teens are sometimes intimidated when they are placed front and center in the midst of adults, it is best if the route of access to the teen space does not require teens to walk through the main adult area of the library. If this type of arrangement is not possible due to the layout of the building, then at least have the furniture arranged so that the walkway to the teen area goes around the primary seating and browsing areas of the adult space.

The teen area should be highly visible for safety and security reasons, yet it should also convey a sense of privacy, so that teens do not feel they are being closely supervised. The area should also provide ready access to important resources and functional areas, so that teens are not required to walk across the adult area to obtain the material and equipment they need to use. Since teens can sometimes be more boisterous than adult library customers, especially when they are working in groups, it is also important that the teen space be acoustically separated from the other areas of the library. Sometimes this may mean having a totally separate room for teens, enclosed by walls, but if the budget is not available for this type of separation, then some type of portable barrier can be used to help mute the sound: such barriers can be in the form of acoustical panels, display cabinets, large plants, curtains, hanging cloth or beads, or free-standing bookshelves.

One technique for deciding upon the location of the teen area is to use a plus/delta process as follows. Place a plus sign at the top of a flipchart or whiteboard. Then leave some space, and place a triangle or delta sign to the right of the plus sign. Vertically, on the left side of the chart or board, library staff and teen planning committee members will brainstorm a list all of the potential locations for the teen library space. Once the list is complete, describe the pluses, or positive and useful ideas for the location, and deltas, or ideas that might need to be re-thought or improved upon for them to work, for each area and write these underneath the appropriate symbol. For example, one of the areas listed could be a back corner of the library directly across from the children's area. A plus for this area might be that it would help to separate the teens from the rest of the library, especially from the children's area. A delta might be that parents who have both young children and teens would have a difficult time supervising them. Once the exercise is complete, examine the list to determine which locations have the most pluses. Those areas would be potential locations for the teen library space. The areas categorized as deltas may have some potential but will more than likely need some type of improvement or change for them to be viable. Of course, the next steps would be to examine the areas more closely to determine which specific one would be best, but the plus/delta exercise is an effective way to begin to narrow choices.

Some additional items to keep in mind when selecting a location for the teen library are as follows:

- Lighting—Both natural and artificial lighting are desirable since the teen space will be used for a variety of functions.
- Electrical outlets—Because teens are heavy technology users, adequate numbers of electrical outlets for computers, TVs and DVD players, data projectors, and other types of equipment are a must.

- Wireless access points—If teens will be using laptop computers, you will not want network cables strung all over the area, so ready access to the Internet using wireless connections is important.
- Flexibility in using the space—More will be said about this.
- Privacy AND visibility—Although teens need to have a sense of privacy, for their safety it is imperative that library staff be able to see teen customers, no matter where they are in the teen library.
- Adequate heating, cooling, and ventilation—Just like adults, teen customers want to feel comfortable in their library, and, just like adults, if they do not, chances are they will not return.
- Easy access to restrooms and water fountains—Teens should not have to walk across the library to use the restroom facilities or get a drink of water, so, if possible, the teen area should be located near these facilities.

ARRANGEMENT

Flexibility is a key element of the teen library space, especially if the area is small. For Kimberley Bolan Taney, one of the most important rules for creating a teen library is that form (or design) must be subordinate to function (or uses) (2003, 10), Large, extravagant artwork items or pervasive high-tech lighting that looks impressive but takes up precious space and causes teen customers to feel cramped when they are trying to complete important homework assignments will not be a practical addition to the space. When planning and designing the arrangement of the teen library, library staff should review the functions of the space and let the floor plan flow from those functions. Even a small space can be attractive and useful if it is arranged according to the activities and functions for which it will be used.

Once the location of the teen space has been determined, start with a blank floor plan, drawn to scale, that can be enlarged and photocopied. Make several copies of this blank plan, and, with the list of functions close at hand, begin to sketch the furniture, equipment, shelving, displays, and other items that will be included in the space. Use a pencil so that changes can easily be made. Draw several different arrangements on the floor plan so that the staff and the teen planning group will have multiple models to review. If a teen area currently exists, draw the layout of this space on one of the blanks so that this can be compared with other versions of the floor plan. There may be certain areas of the current teen library that should not be rearranged, and this comparison will help staff and teens to quickly see such areas.

If possible, instead of simply drawing various arrangements on the floor plans, make cutouts of all of the furniture, equipment, shelving, and other items that will be included in the teen space. You can easily move the cutouts to different locations to see how various arrangements will look. The cutouts can also be color coded so that staff and teens can easily see exactly what types of items are located in specific places. This activity is quite useful when staff members are planning the teen space, and it is enjoyable to move things around and get an immediate concrete, visual sense of how each model floor plan will look. A hint on tables: generally, square tables are more versatile than round or rectangular tables as they can be arranged in a variety of ways.

CONTENTS OF THE TEEN LIBRARY

As with other considerations for the teen library, the furniture and equipment to be included will largely be determined by the functions or activities that will occur there. In general, the teen library will include such basic items as worktables and chairs, comfortable chairs or couches, end tables and reading lamps, individual study carrels or booths, display cases, bulletin boards, paperback racks, computers (the more, the better), computer tables and chairs, media racks, book shelving, viewing/listening equipment and areas, shelving for reference/research material such as atlases, dictionary stands, book display areas, circulation desk or self-checkout computers, and perhaps an area for speakers or presentations such as musical performances. Decorative items such as special lighting, life-size cardboard cutouts of celebrities, reading nooks, recording booths, or others can be added once the basic arrangement and contents are finalized.

DÉCOR

Deciding upon how to enhance and decorate the teen library is the fun part of the planning process! At this phase of planning, staff and teen planners should "go shopping" for ideas by visiting other popular teen hangouts and teen libraries. As visits are made, staff and teen planners should make lists of ideas and concepts that they like, as well as ones that they do not like. Then the planning team can get together to discuss considerations such as the following:

- The overall look and feel that is desired
- Colors for both decorative items and wall paint
- Specific types of lighting
- Exact style of furniture, including tables, chairs, displays, shelving, and so on
- Fabric patterns
- Décor for special areas such as a coffee bar or café, gaming area, or homework center
- Decorative items that could be included, such as sculpture, posters, paintings, three-dimensional art or nature objects, bulletin boards, pillows, plants, magnetic word walls or poetry, clocks, tube lighting, life-size cardboard cutouts of celebrities or characters, rugs, and other items

If the planning team is struggling with making decisions about these items, it may be helpful to decide upon a basic theme for the teen library first, and then begin to identify the types of decorative items that are needed to illustrate the theme. One note of caution: unless the library has a large, ongoing source of funding, be careful of selecting a theme or decorative items that may be time sensitive. If the theme is based upon something that may be popular today but out of style next year, it will be quite costly to keep the teen library up to date. Try not to base the teen library's theme on popular movies, characters, books, TV shows, or the like. For example, a theme such as "The Manga Meeting Place," based on one of the popular genres of graphic novels, is much more likely to go out of vogue than a more generic theme like "The Teen Spot" or something of that nature. Teens do like slogans, so selecting a theme that can be announced and prominently displayed at the entry of the teen library is highly appealing. As with every other step of the planning process, teens should definitely be involved in selecting the theme for their library space.

A LEVEL-BASED PLANNING APPROACH

The Concept

If funding and support are not in place to create a complete, fully functioning teen library, then a level-based or phased-in approach may be needed. Basically, the idea is to put together a plan in which three levels are included—minimal, adequate, and awesome. The staff and teen planners would then identify the components of each of these levels, complete with estimated costs. As additional funding and support become available, the teen library could evolve to the next level, with an ultimate goal of achieving an exemplary teen library within, say, three to five years. Each library's planning group will have its own idea of what should be included at each of the three levels, but some considerations and guidelines are provided below.

The Minimal Teen Library Space

A basic/minimal teen library space may simply consist of a corner somewhere within the adult library in which a small YA collection is housed. Along with a small collection of YA fiction books, this area could include the following:

- One OPAC (online public access computer, that is, a computer containing the electronic card catalog)
- One computer for Internet access, a periodical research database, and word-processing software
- One networked printer
- One small worktable with four chairs

- A couple of comfy chairs or a sofa
- Two or three teen magazines displayed on a coffee table or end table
- A small collection of "ready reference" material such as a dictionary, a set of encyclopedias, a world almanac, and an atlas
- Minimal decorative items such as celebrity posters, a colorful wall or banner, and an interesting reading lamp or small neon light fixture

Even a basic teen area such as this one can be organized around some type of theme that can be exemplified by posters, signage, and book displays. Despite the small size and limited amount of furnishings, materials, and equipment, a well-planned basic teen space can be appealing and functional, and it can make teen customers feel that they have their own special place in the library.

The Adequate Teen Library Space

Of course, having a larger teen space will allow the library to provide more services and resources to teen customers. Rather than simply being located in a small corner of the adult library area, the average or adequate teen space could be a slightly larger area that is in a totally separate room from the rest of the library or is separated from it by acoustical panels that can be decorated on the teen library side so that they are both functional and attractive. In addition to the items mentioned for the basic teen space, the average space could include the following:

- One additional OPAC
- One additional research computer, with both of the research computers providing Internet access, an electronic periodicals database, electronic databases for each of the major subject areas, and word-processing software
- One or two additional tables for group projects
- A browsing area with comfy furniture, and magazines displayed on magazine shelving
- One book display area with popular fiction titles
- Additional print reference materials such as specialized dictionaries, Opposing Viewpoints series books for speech and debate classes, and other high-demand print resources
- Additional decorative visual items, as well as interesting lighting and art objects

The Awesome Teen Library Space

This level refers to the "if money were no object" teen library. While rare in today's times of tight budgets, an exemplary/awesome teen library could evolve over time if the adult community believes that a teen library is critical, and is willing to fund it. The teen library would be housed in a room that is totally separate from the rest of the library, with adequate space for all of the above items, but with additional furniture, equipment, and collection resources to meet the needs of larger numbers of teens. Although function would still outweigh form, much more could be included in the way of decorative lighting and visuals, and access to technology would be ubiquitous. A few items that could be considered for inclusion in an exemplary teen library are listed here:

- A presentation area for speakers or musical performances
- A surround sound–type theater
- A video production studio and relevant equipment
- Computer presentation centers at which teens could create PowerPoint™ slideshows, computer-based video presentations, podcasts, and other high-tech products
- A full-service coffee bar or café
- A teen bookstore
- A computer-assisted design (CAD) center
- A full computer lab with multiple functions

Even if it is not possible for your library to develop an exemplary teen space at the present time, it is always a good idea to have a vision of what could be done if money were unlimited. Who knows, there may be someone in your community who has a passion for serving the needs of young adults and bequeaths a substantial amount of money to the library for just this purpose. Or the members of your library board may decide that the teen library should be a priority, in which case they would be willing to lead a fund-raising effort to develop it. No matter whether these speculations are realistic or not, it is always an excellent idea to maintain a vision for your teen library, as this will motivate the library staff to continue to improve both the services and facilities for teens in your community.

TIPS AND REMINDERS

As you begin the planning process for the teen library, you should consider some final issues and reminders:

- Include teens throughout the planning process.
- Start with a needs assessment of some type.
- Based on the results of the needs assessment, decide upon the specific functions/purposes that the teen library will fulfill and be mindful of this throughout the planning process.
- Ask questions from time to time, such as: What will it look like? Who will it serve? Who needs to be involved? What is our timeframe? Who is responsible for what? and other questions that will help your planning group stay focused.

- Develop a timeline for each phase of the project.
- Make sure that along with the plan for the library space, you also have a long- and short-term plan for teen library services. The two go together.

Not only should teens be involved in the planning process, but they also should be involved in the implementation of various initiatives by making contributions and providing input. Teens can participate in many ways, such as creating teen artwork to decorate the space; suggesting teen projects and programs to be offered; making requests about popular fiction to be purchased; assisting staff in preparing book displays and bulletin boards; contributing peer book reviews; preparing lists of popular books, movies, TV shows, celebrities, and other teen favorites that can be included on signs, brochures, or bookmarks; and other many other items that directly affect them as library customers. Teens will own their space if they are continually involved in and consulted on issues that impact them.

Finally, think of the teen library as a journey rather than a destination, as it will need to be constantly changing to meet the needs and desires of teen customers. This does not mean that a major makeover must occur often, but it is important to make minor changes continually, so that teens never know what to expect when they enter their library and are continually curious about what's coming next. This type of variety and surprise makes the teen library dynamic! Making such minor changes as putting up new posters frequently; providing different, attractive bookmarks from time to time; making available brochures on upcoming projects, contests, and programs; displaying new teen artwork; rearranging furniture; and rotating book displays will make the teen library continually engaging and interesting to its customers.

A WORD ABOUT STAFFING

Although it may seem obvious, those who staff the teen library MUST like teens! The fastest way to kill your teen library program is to staff the teen library with someone who is either intimidated by or hostile toward teens. If the library budget does not include money for hiring a trained teen librarian, or if you are in a one-person library in which you serve all of your customers, then it is imperative for you to take the initiative to learn more about teens and their needs for library services. You may have to do some additional research on working with teens, but this does not have to involve formal education. One way to learn more about teens is to ask for assistance from those who regularly work with them, including high school teachers, high school librarians, church staff members who teach teens, people who work with teens at the local YMCA, and community leaders who work with teen groups such as Boy Scouts or Girl Scouts.

Many collegial networks exist, and some of them will be discussed in chapter 7. The most important criterion for successfully working with teens is simply the desire to do it. If you have no such desire and do not have funding to hire a specialist in this area, then seek volunteers in the community who DO enjoy working with teens and are willing to donate some time to assist you in providing teen services in the library.

WEB RESOURCES

Betwixt and Between: http://www.libraryjournal.com/article/CA63 96445.html—an article from *Library Journal,* featuring a compilation of statistical information on 160 library-building projects, as well as a listing of architectural firms throughout the United States.

MHLS: Library Space Planning, Children's and Teen's Areas: http://midhudson.org/ department/youth/Space_PlanningYS.htm—this contains a wealth of information on various aspects of planning teen library spaces, including a list of suppliers of various items for the teen library and a list of furniture vendors.

WebJunction's Focus on Space Planning for Libraries: http://webjunction.org/do/ DisplayContent?id=12748—this includes a variety of topics and suggestions for planning library facilities.

CHAPTER 7

The Three Ps

Just like all other professions in today's split-second, information-driven world, the library profession changes rapidly. Thus, it is important to stay abreast of changes and continue to offer up-do-date resources, programs, and services to your customers, especially your teen customers. The days of quiet libraries with warehouses of books are long past. Today's library customers want current, high-tech information resources, ubiquitous computing ability, and a popular books collection that changes as often as the *New York Times* best seller list. Thus, professional growth is imperative if your teen library is to be viewed by its customers as an essential resource.

While years ago the library may not have had numerous competitors for the resources and services it offered, today's library is constantly vying for customers' patronage because of such facilities as mega bookstores, retail video rental stores, cable and satellite TV, gaming arcades, and the huge number of home computers in our country. Our citizenry now has access to the Internet with its plethora of online bookstores and malls like Amazon.com, free Web sites and reference resources, and many other items that were once almost exclusively the purview of the public library. Therefore, attending conferences and staff development workshops, keeping up with professional reading, and networking with professional colleagues are no longer luxuries. Instead, your teen customers (and others!) expect that those who work in public libraries will be cutting edge information providers, continually learning and growing.

This chapter will give you some tools and tips for staying current in your profession as well as promoting the current and new services that your library has to offer. As the old saying goes, "if you are standing still, you are going backwards," Another way to say this is that "the only constant is change": all of us who work in library environments must learn to be change agents and salespersons. To keep our public libraries viable and relevant means to serve the needs of our teen customers, as well as all of our other customers.

PROFESSIONAL RESOURCES

Many professional resources exist for librarians. In fact, it can be overwhelming to sift and sort through the wealth of information available. The material discussed below will provide a starting place to help you access some professional resources that offer practical and affordable means to meet your needs. Start small by selecting a few resources until you gain more experience and learn what will best meet your needs. Remember also that there are many free resources on the World Wide Web, so if your budget is tight, begin with those, making sure to look for tools that are authoritative and credible. Also, do not forget that some of your most valuable resources may be your colleagues, so form good relationships early on with those in the library profession that you consider to be knowledgeable and experienced.

Journals

Here is a list of various journals with information on publishers and brief descriptions. Pricing and ordering information can be obtained by contacting the publishers or magazine jobbers such as EBSCO or Cox Periodicals.

- *American Libraries* (published by the American Library Association/ALA) features articles about the library profession, columns on miscellaneous topics of interest, news and current events related to libraries, job listings, information on PR and advocacy, and the organization's political initiatives on issues that impact the profession.
- *Booklist* (published by the ALA), as the title implies, contains annotated lists of all types of books and other media with critical reviews of material for all types of libraries, written by public librarians and school library media specialists.
- *Library Journal* (published by Reed Business Information) combines news, features, commentary, public policy analysis, information on technology, and reports on management developments of interest to those in the library profession who work in public libraries.

- *School Library Journal* (published by Reed Business Information), despite its title, includes articles of interest to both public and school librarians who work with youth and teens; it contains reviews of all types of material from children's and teen books to professional books and other resources.
- *Voice of Youth Advocates (VOYA)* (published by Scarecrow Press) contains articles of interest to teen librarians and secondary school library media specialists; it includes reviews of all types of materials for teen collections.

Electronic Discussion Lists

Several Internet-based discussion lists are available; some of these are quite broad in focus, with literally hundreds of members, and others are narrower in focus, with a more limited number of members and contributors. If you do not have time to actively "post" to lists, then subscribe to the "digest" format that provides brief summaries of messages. This will allow you to quickly skim the postings and decide which ones to read and which ones to delete.

The PUBLIB Electronic Discussion List is geared to public library staff, and it includes online discussions of such areas as collection development and management, reference services, facilities, library policy, trustee issues, intellectual freedom, personnel issues, and more. Information about subscribing can be found at http://lists.webjunction.org/publib/. The list was founded in 1992, and it is the oldest list of its type for public library staff.

YALSA offers several electronic discussion lists that are specifically directed to teen library staff. To get more information or subscribe to a specific list, go to http://www.ala.org/yalsa/professional/yalsalists.html.

The lists mentioned below are sponsored by the ALA. There is no subscription fee, and you can unsubscribe from the lists easily if you decide that they do not offer what you need. All of these Internet discussion lists can be subscribed to by sending a message to the ALA's electronic discussion list management site. Simply send a message to: LISTPROC@ALA.ORG, leaving the subject line blank and including the following in the body of your message: subscribe [listname] [YourFirstName] [Your LastName].

- PR Talk features sharing of ideas on promotion and marketing for your library (list name: prtalk).
- Library Advocacy Now! offers ideas and updates on legislative issues affecting libraries (list name: aladnow).
- @ your library™ contains topics and updates regarding the advocacy campaign titled "The Campaign for America's Libraries" (list name: campaign).
- ALA News Releases provides users with an online copy of the ALA's news (list name: alanews).

- The Washington Office Electronic Newsline sends important legislative information to users (list name: alawon).

Collegial Networks

As I mentioned earlier, people can be tremendous resources for those teen librarians who are just starting out in the profession. Although formal networks do exist, sometimes an informal network of exemplary professionals can be just as effective in providing needed support and information. Thus, it is important to quickly learn who your peers are, contact them, and begin to establish good working relationships. The library profession as a whole is characterized by sharing, so most librarians are very receptive to helping novices by sharing ideas, resources, and expertise. One caution: be sure to look to those teen librarians who understand and model best practices in the field. This means that you need to do some creative eavesdropping to discover who these folks are. Also, watch your peers in meetings, at workshops, and at conferences to determine who the respected leaders are. Then seek out these people and learn from them. Also, make sure to give something back to your mentors rather than only taking from them. Simple expressions of thanks via small gifts, recommending these folks for paid speaking engagements, nominating them for various awards, and inviting them to be your guests for coffee or a meal are all nice ways to acknowledge your appreciation.

In addition to informal networks, formal networks can be valuable to your professional growth. These networks can be local, regional, or statewide. You can usually find out about these networks by simply asking someone who has been around for a while. Such people can direct you to those who can tell you how to get involved.

If by chance there is no informal or formal network available within reasonable proximity to you, then start your own. There may be other teen librarians just like you who are seeking a professional support group, so do not be afraid to be the initiator of a collegial network in your area. It may be that your network will be composed of school librarians, public librarians, and community college librarians, all of whom work with teens. Although there are some differences among types of librarians, we have much in common, so if you are the only public librarian who works with teens in your community, reach out to your colleagues who work in other types of libraries. You will all benefit from the conversation and idea sharing that develops over time.

Library Publishers

The following list includes publishers who publish professional books for librarians. Check the publishers' Web sites to find lists of titles, descriptions of books, authors, pricing and ordering information, and other information.

The American Library Association (ALA) (http://www.ala.org) provides books and periodicals for library and information professionals, as well as promotional and decorative items such as posters, bookmarks, and so forth. As mentioned previously, the ALA also publishes *American Libraries,* a professional journal for those working in all types of libraries.

Libraries Unlimited (http://www.lu.com), part of the Greenwood Publishing Group, publishes bibliographies, reference books, library science textbooks, information science materials, and handbooks and manuals for practicing librarians, library educators, media specialists, and teachers. Libraries Unlimited also produces an excellent database on genre fiction that is available via subscription, as was indicated in chapter 4 of this book.

Linworth Publishing, Inc. (http://linworth.com) publishes practitioner-focused materials in three different lines: Linworth Books, which produces professional books for school library media specialists and children's and teen librarians; Linworth Learning, which includes activity-based books for classroom teachers; and Library Media Connection (LMC), which is a professional magazine for K–12 school library media specialists, technology specialists, and public library youth and teen librarians.

Neal Schuman Publishers, Inc. (http://nealschuman.com) publishes professional resources for several groups: librarians and library educators, library students, educators, and researchers. Their how-to-do-it manuals provide basic, foundational information on all aspects of managing and maintaining libraries.

Scarecrow Press (http://scarecrowpress.com), part of the Rowan & Littlefield Publishing Group, is known for scholarly bibliographies and library science monographs.

Your State Library

The state library has been mentioned previously in various contexts. Each state has its own library department, which provides a multitude of services and resources. Most state libraries employ consultants or specialists in each library area, including the areas of school libraries, public libraries, and academic libraries. Sometimes the state library is affiliated with the state department of education, so start there to obtain specific information.

State libraries typically provide a wide range of materials and services to assist librarians in their professional growth efforts. Your state library will more than likely offer workshops and training sessions on a variety of topics and in a variety of locations throughout the state. Some state libraries also sponsor an electronic discussion list for librarians. Take advantage of training opportunities as they are offered, as some are either free or provided at nominal cost. Also, contact the state library consultant for public libraries to learn more about programs (such as a teen summer reading program) that directly apply to public libraries throughout your state.

Your state may also have regional organizations that provide staff development training and resources. The state library will be able to tell you what types of state and regionally sponsored professional growth opportunities are available, and their staff can give you necessary contact information to help you enroll in workshops and receive material.

PROFESSIONAL GROWTH

It has been said that most people will change jobs or careers at least seven times during their lifetimes. For many people who are moving to a different career, little to no formal training is provided. This may have been the case when you became a teen librarian or started working with teens as a public library staff member. If this is true of your situation, then you will find that it is up to you to learn about your profession and continue to grow professionally. In addition to using the professional resources, services, and networks mentioned above, you will also need to employ some other strategies to help you continue to grow. Some tips for success in your professional growth initiatives are given below.

- Do not assume that "someone will help me learn about my new job." Take the initiative to learn about your profession in active ways.
- Know what your professional growth goals are, and set new ones every year.
- Prepare a written professional growth plan and include relevant topics such as collection development, technology, public services, technical services, programming, reference services, readers' advisory, and other areas in which you need to improve or progress.
- Keep a professional journal. This single tool can help you more than any other as you continue to grow professionally. Be reflective about what you are doing and how you are doing it. Write in this journal on a daily basis, and use it to develop a professional growth plan for success.
- Be a teen library "sponge," soaking up everything you can about your profession by taking notes, watching people, and listening to those with more experience than you.
- Learn about the current research that undergirds your profession. Many statistical and anecdotal studies can help you learn through others' efforts. Your state library can provide information on these studies.
- Find a mentor or mentors, and establish an ongoing professional relationship with this person or group.
- Make sure to recognize and thank those who have helped you professionally.
- Read, read, read about your profession!
- Continue to look for and attend conferences, workshops, meetings, and other events that will contribute to your professional growth.
- Join your professional organizations, and be an active member.

- Never be satisfied with the status quo. Libraries are ever-changing organisms, so always look forward and never bemoan the passing of the "good old days" of the past.

Professional Organizations

The ALA is our "mother" organization, and it provides a plethora of resources and services to librarians in all areas of the library profession. As you move down through the organization, you will discover more specific groups that meet more narrowly defined needs. The ALA currently has 11 divisions, each of which focuses on a type of library or type of library function (such as teen services). Divisions such as the Public Library Association (PLA) and YALSA have been developed to meet some of the more specific needs. Although the dues payable to the ALA and its divisions can be a bit expensive, the benefits are well worth the cost! If you are not currently a member of our national organization, you should join immediately. Ask your supervisor or board members if funding is available to pay all or a portion of the dues. If this has not been done in the past, be sure to do some homework before you request funding. You should be able to clearly articulate the benefits that will accrue to your library as a result of your membership.

The PLA is a very active division of the ALA, with its own blog, Web site, conference, and many other resources. The PLA conference is an invaluable event designed to help library staff in all areas stay current and learn about new, cutting-edge developments in public library resources and services. Find further information on the ALA's website; click on "Our Association," "Divisions," and "PLA."

YALSA is the most specifically focused division for those who are teen librarians. Like the PLA, YALSA has a wealth of resources and services for those who work with teens in libraries. Although YALSA does not sponsor its own conference, it does sponsor many workshops and sessions at both the ALA and PLA conferences. In addition, YALSA provides information on teen reading, award-winning teen books, Teen Tech Week, and other news and events of interest to teen librarians. YALSA also sponsors several online courses for teen librarians. The cost of each course is reasonable, and the instructors are well-known and respected experts in their areas. Topics include such items as readers' advisory, adolescent development and behavior, teen programming, and electronic databases of interest to teens.

All states have a state professional library organization that is affiliated with the ALA. The dues are typically lower than those of the ALA and its divisions, so the services are more limited. However, most professional growth materials and events are geared more specifically to areas that impact the libraries and librarians in your state, so there is more of a local emphasis. State professional organizations usually have an annual conference, and some organizations also provide regional workshops and training. If you simply cannot afford to join the ALA, then join your state organization and set a goal of joining the ALA within a certain time period. Just as the ALA publishes a professional journal, so do some state organizations. This journal should be included with your membership. Your state organization may also include smaller groups that hold meetings and training workshops for those working in a specific type of library. Contact your state library for information on the professional organizations in your state.

Free or Inexpensive Staff Development Resources

If your library does not have funding to subscribe to the professional journals mentioned previously or to purchase professional books, then ask your state library about free or inexpensive materials that it provides. Utilize the Web resources listed in this book to help you continue to grow professionally. You can also ask your mentors and others who work with teens in libraries about resources that are affordable. As you find excellent resources, both print and electronic, save them to file folders or bookmark them on your computer, so that you have ready access to them when you need them in the future. Arrange the resources by topic, then by date, with the most recent dates in the front of the file or at the top of your bookmarks, from newest to oldest. Just as you weed the collection in your teen library, be sure to weed these resources also. Otherwise you will run out of space and you may find yourself using resources that are seriously out of date.

Conferences and Workshops

As has already been indicated, most of the professional organizations that you join will offer conferences and training workshops. Attend the annual conferences of the state and national organizations if at all possible. Select regional and local workshops as needed to gain information on rapidly changing topics, such as new technologies for libraries. If you cannot attend the national or state conferences, then make sure to debrief with a colleague who does attend these conferences to find out the most important things she or he has learned. Sometimes presenters' handouts from conferences or workshops are posted on the Web sites of the organizations afterward. Check with your professional organizations to find out if this is done. Then, go to the relevant Web site to look for handouts on topics of interest or need.

While conference attendance is important, it can sometimes be overwhelming, due to all of the preparation and follow-up required to maximize the experience. Some tips for making the most of the conference experience are given below:

- Be sure to register as early as is possible, since many organizations offer a discounted rate for early registration.
- Keep all conference documents in an envelope or folder of some type. You may need to change or cancel your room or travel reservation, so it is imperative that you have the appropriate documents handy and well organized. Also, your

library will require some financial documents to verify each expense, so keep all receipts and itemized invoices.

- Be sure to make hotel and travel arrangements early. Hotels for national conferences book up quickly, so unless you want to take a 30-minute bus ride to the conference center and back to your hotel several times a day, book early to get accommodations in the "conference hotel," which is typically the one closest to the conference center.

- If you plan to attend any special meals or similar events at the conference, you will need additional funds, besides those for registration, to pay for these events.

- Many vendors use early registration lists to obtain contact information in order to send out ad pieces prior to the conference. If you receive these, determine which ones you are interested in, and keep them in an envelope or file, along with your other conference documents. Organize vendor information by topic or date so that you have a plan listing the vendor booths you will visit or the vendor presentations you will attend. Throw away vendor information in which you are not interested.

- Go to the conference Web site to get a preliminary program. Download and print the program if possible. Mark the events and sessions that you plan to attend, so that you will have a daily schedule to follow. If you wait until you arrive at the conference to decide what to attend, you will find that you spend an inordinate amount of time reading program descriptions: this wastes time that could be spent actually attending sessions.

- Be sure to take business cards with you, as many vendors have drawings for free materials and services. Rather than spending time filling out registration cards for these items, simply drop your business card in the box or other container.

- Just as you decide what events and sessions to attend in advance of the conference, you should, as mentioned above, also develop a preliminary plan listing the vendors' booths you want to visit. Typically, vendors are listed in the back of the program with a number indicating their location in the exhibits hall. Circle the numbers of the vendor booths or make a list of them, and plan your approach to visiting the exhibits hall. If the conference is very large, like the ALA conference, you may want to go to the exhibits hall several times, visiting a limited number of vendor booths each time.

- Dress at conferences can be quite varied. Business casual is usually appropriate, unless you are making a presentation, in which case you will want to dress up a bit more. You may not need to wear suits and ties if you are a guy or heels and hose if you are a woman, but you do need to look professional: no jeans, sweats, or jogging suits except in your room. No matter what other clothes you wear, be sure to wear shoes that are comfortable and have good arch support. Purchasing a new pair of shoes immediately before a conference (and wearing them at the conference) is suicidal!

- When you register at a conference, you should receive a conference badge and program, along with a variety of other items. Your conference badge is your admission to the exhibits hall and to conference sessions and other events. Wear it and keep it visible at all times.

- Your conference program is an invaluable tool that includes a complete guide to all sessions and programs, maps of the conference center, lists of conference hotels and contact information, and information on the exhibits hall and conference center layout, the list of vendors, special organizational meetings, and other items. Keep the program with you at all times, and consult it first when you have questions.

- Most conferences have information booths available, so look for these when you have questions about matters such as local sites to see and events to attend, places to dine, and directions to shopping areas or other locations.

- If you are attending the conference with a group of colleagues, decide in advance what sessions you will all attend, and try not to duplicate your attendance at the same sessions. This way you can all share information, when you return home, in a kind of mini staff development workshop format. You can also invite to your workshop the people who were unable to attend the conference.

- Although notepads may be furnished in your registration packet, it is always a good idea to take your own notepad or portfolio. You may not want to write on the handouts provided by a presenter, so taking your own paper is a good idea.

- If you need to leave a session before it ends, do so discreetly. I like to sit at the end of a row so that I do not disturb others if I have to leave.

- Remember to be polite and respectful during a presentation—whether you are interested in the topic or not! It is extremely rude to talk or whisper with a colleague while a presenter is speaking. Who knows, that presenter may just be someone you will work for or with at some time in the future.

- Conferences provide tremendous opportunities to network with colleagues and meet folks from whom you can learn and with whom you can share. Do not stay isolated in your room at the end of the day. May a plan to network with colleagues at every chance and meet at least one new person each day. Be sure to exchange business cards. Follow up with these people shortly after the conference.

- When you return from a conference, immediately organize your notes and handouts. Otherwise, they will sit in a stack or file gathering dust. Set up files of handouts and notes by topic and date, just as you do with your professional reading materials. Also, review these within 24 hours of the conference to help reinforce what you have learned.

- Discard the handouts that you will truly never need or use. Otherwise, they will simply take up valuable space in your professional growth files.

- Find one idea, strategy, or program to implement immediately upon returning to your library, and do it!

- Schedule the ideas, strategies, or programs that you plan to implement by putting them on your calendar or a dated "to do" list. Include a brief description of how you plan to implement the ideas, so that they you will remember important details.
- Complete your expense reports and any other reports to your supervisor or board as soon as possible. Sometimes unusual expenses may occur, and you will need to provide an explanation for them. If you wait even for a few days, you may forget about these expenses and then not be able to justify them. The same is true of programs or meetings on which you need to give a report.

Professional Reading

Much has been said about this already. However, it bears emphasizing that you must continually read professional articles, books, newsletters, meeting notes, and other items to stay abreast of issues and information in the area of teen library services. Use professional journals to read reviews of professional books, and select titles that match your needs. Once you start reading professional materials, you will begin to identify authors whom you respect. Develop a file or list of those authors and their areas of expertise, so that you can look for new titles as they are produced.

Because there is an almost unlimited amount of professional resource material available, concentrate on reading material in the areas that you are weakest in as well as those areas that are a focus of your library's mission, vision, and strategic plan. If no such documents exist for your library, be instrumental in developing them, so that the library has a direction and plan for improvement. Share expensive books and other items with your collegial network so that no one bears the cost alone. Use interlibrary loan services throughout your region or state to find materials to check out rather than purchasing every title. Start a professional book club or discussion group with your peers and mentors. If distance does not allow you to meet physically, then circulate a book or article among your group via e-mail, mail, or courier service and schedule a time for an online discussion about it.

Do not feel compelled to read every word of every professional article or book. With regard to professional journals, read the table of contents first, to select articles that you want to read in their entirety. Then, skim the other articles or, if you have absolutely no interest in or need for the information presented in an article, skip it entirely. Photocopy articles or sections of articles to which you will want to refer in the future. For example, if you will be planning next year's programs soon, you might want to photocopy an article with excellent program ideas and refer to it when you begin to plan.

When reading professional books, read the table of contents first, then skim the index. Write down topics and page numbers from both that identity material you want to examine further. If you are looking for very specific information on a topic, read only the specifically relevant sections. If you are seeking general knowledge about a topic, you may want to read an entire chapter or book. As you read, highlight sections, flag pages, take notes, or do a combination of all of these so that you can easily refer to the resource in the future as needs occur. As with articles, photocopy those pages that you find to be most valuable. Organize the material according to topic and date for easy future use.

PUBLIC RELATIONS AND MARKETING

Although these two areas go hand in hand and share some characteristics, they are not totally the same. Public relations has to do with establishing positive relationships with all of the stakeholders and customers of your library. Marketing focuses specifically on "selling" what your library has to offer, including all programs, resources, and services. One certainly impacts the other, however. If, for example, you have a nasty conflict with the high school librarian in your community, you may find that when you ask to present your teen summer reading program to students, you are prevented from marketing this program because of the ill will that has been created. On the other hand, if you have established an excellent working relationship with high school librarians, you may find not only that they are willing to have you come to the school and present the program to students but that they are willing to help you schedule, set up, and deliver your presentations. Thus, both public relations and marketing are critical to the ongoing well-being of the teen library program.

You Are the Face of the Library!

Here is a mental exercise to help you fully grasp this concept. Do a mental visualization. Take a minute to think about each of the following: your bank, your grocery store, your pharmacy, the dry cleaner you use, the auto repair shop you frequent, your favorite restaurants, your neighborhood post office, and your hairstylist. As you thought about each one of these places, what mental picture came into your head? Did you think about the tools the auto repair shop uses, the aisles in the grocery store, and the size and shape of the drive-in window at the bank, or did you think about the people you encounter at each of these places? Chances are, you thought about the people. Just as you thought of the people at the places you frequent, so do your library's teen and adult customers think about you and the other people who assist them when they go to the library. The power you have to influence your customers' attitudes and opinions about the library is staggering! What you say and how you behave in all the situations in your life in which you come in contact with people can potentially impact the opinion that all these people have of the library. Thus, although your library may not have lots of money to play for slick PR and marketing programs, you CAN be a professional, positive, public figure as you interface with community members each day and greatly influence their opinions about the public library.

In addition to making sure that you are positive in your attitude and behavior when you come in contact with members of the community, you can also make a positive impression by being knowledgeable about the programs and services offered by your library. For example, when you visit a local high school to talk about the teen summer reading program, be prepared to answer questions on whether the library has a particular new book on the best seller list or on the policies regarding e-mail accounts and chat rooms. Every person you meet is a potential library supporter or library critic, so use your public "face" to promote active support for the library.

Your Library's Customers

As was mentioned previously, literally all the people in your community are customers of the library. They may not be active, participating customers who use the library on a regular basis, but they are taxpaying community members who can vote for or against important bond or budget initiatives. These external customers are to be found everywhere in your community, so in addition to maintaining good public relations, it is also a good idea to learn and practice your "elevator speech" or "script" about the library, both the library as a whole and the teen library specifically. Your elevator speech or script is a short (no more than a couple of minutes) talk that you give verbally to folks with whom you come into contact who may not know much about the library. You will want to cover the most important resources, services, and programs that the library provides, as well as giving the location of the library and the necessary contact information. Try not to have more than about five to seven points you want to convey. Know your facts. If you are asked a question that you cannot answer, do not fake it. Take the person's name and contact information, and say you will find out the information. Then do just that, and try to get back to the person within a few days. Be sure to carry a business card that includes your name, the library's address, the main phone number of the library, and the library Web site's URL.

Most of us are familiar with our external customers and have at least a basic understanding of who they are, but we may not be quite as familiar with our internal customers. Your internal customers are those people who are affiliated in some way with the library, people with whom you have some type of professional relationship and with whom you come into contact. They may include library staff members, board members, volunteers, teen library advisory board members, pages, or Friends of the Library members. Just as you seek to establish and maintain good relationships with your external customers, it is imperative to do the same with your library's internal customers. Your teen library advisory board members, for example, can be powerful advocates and promoters of the library, so you will want to maintain a positive attitude toward the library when you work with members of this group. Always emphasize the good things that are going on with regard to the teen library and provide lots of information that group members can share with their peers.

Some simple strategies to promote your library and continue to provide excellent customer service are listed below:

- Memorize and use your library script whenever appropriate.
- Talk about the library at every opportunity, but be careful not to overdo it. Not everyone is as passionate about the library as you are, especially teens.
- Keep a list of your internal and external customers, and strive to improve relationships with the people on both lists.
- If you have a conflict with someone outside or inside the library, try not to make it personal. Speak to the issue and not to the person's behavior or personal attributes.
- Always have a "can do" attitude. This means when you have to tell someone "no," always suggest what you CAN do for them.
- Do not promise what you cannot fulfill. This will only lead to ill will later and will give the impression that the library is NOT responsive to customers' needs.
- Know your limits. If you continually extend yourself beyond your abilities or time, you will at some point become resentful. No one likes a martyr, so make sure that you set reasonable limits to the services you provide.
- Set priorities. You cannot possibly do everything, so it is imperative that you have a clear understanding of those things that need to rise to the top of the pile and those things that can and must wait.
- Finally, take care of yourself, mentally, physically, and spiritually. Nurture yourself so that you can better serve others.

The bottom line in public relations is that you must always practice the "p" word, politics, whenever possible with both your internal and your external customers. Positive politics leads to positive PR that leads to your customers feeling a positive sense of place when they visit the library. The word "public" says it all when it comes to PR and marketing for the library.

Creating Material to Market Your Library

Unless you have a marketing or development director for your library, you may be called upon to create marketing tools for the teen library program. If so, you will first need to become familiar with software programs such as Microsoft Word™, Microsoft Publisher™, or other desktop publishing programs, and then learn some basics about designing material. Just as with all other areas, there are many resources that can help you, the first of which are your teen library advisory board members. Some of them will either have expertise in creating marketing material or will know other teens who are experts in this area. Once you decide upon the basic information that needs to be included on a flier or brochure, for example, ask your teen customers to help you produce the material.

Other excellent resources for marketing material are your professional organizations. Both the ALA and YALSA have excellent examples of ad slogans, brochures, and other marketing tools on their Web sites. Use the tools on these sites as a starting place, and customize them to fit the needs of your library. Your state library will also have examples of marketing materials that you can obtain or adapt to your needs.

In addition to your teen customers and professional organizations, it is likely that someone in your library's Friends group or volunteer group has talent in graphic design. Place an ad on your library's Web site or bulletin board seeking assistance in this area. Make sure to ask for samples of the person's work before asking her or him to assist you. Just as you want to display a positive, professional demeanor as the face of your library, you want your PR and marketing tools to be of high quality and professionally produced. If this means that you must limit the production of these items due to a restricted budget, then do so. Less is sometimes more in this respect, meaning that your customers will have a better impression of the library if they receive fewer but higher-quality PR pieces from the library than if they are inundated with tons of library fliers, brochures, and the like that are poorly prepared and produced. The days of "black and white" are gone. Whenever possible, your marketing tools should be in full color, or at least in multiple colors.

Writing Press Releases

Press releases can be formulaic. Before you attempt to write a press release about a program that your library has given or is going to give, contact your local newspapers to find out whether they have a specific format they prefer or require. If not, contact the local school district, hospital, city government offices, or other large organization in your area to ask if they have a sample press release they would be willing to share with you.

If none of these local organizations can provide you with a template for a press release, contact your state library. The following are some tips to keep in mind:

- Before writing a press release, make sure to ask, "Is this event/resource/information newsworthy?" If not, do not waste your time or anyone else's by writing a press release.
- If possible, find a special angle for your press release. A mundane approach will not seduce readers and make them want to learn more. Be creative in your approach.
- Make sure that you are clear about the purpose for the press release. It should have a major point to make rather than being a collection of random events or ideas.
- Use consistent formatting throughout the press release.
- Make sure that the press release is timely. Old news should be covered in some other format than a press release.

- Make the press release concise. Include brief accounts of facts rather than lots of descriptive narrative.
- Be sure to give accurate attribution to others and distinguish between opinions and facts.
- Be sure to have someone review the press release and check it for accuracy, grammar, and spelling before you submit it.
- If approval is required, make sure to obtain it prior to sending the press release.

Your Praise File

We all have days on which we question why we are doing what we do professionally. This can certainly be the case for those working with teens in libraries! Just as you may not have anyone to provide technical training for you to help you learn how to be a teen librarian, you may not receive many compliments on a job well done. Thus, when you DO receive "pats on the back," whether physical, written, or verbal, it is important to preserve them and refer to them on those days when it all goes wrong. Create a professional praise file in which you place thank you notes or commendations given to you by others, as well as journal entries that you have made when you receive verbal compliments. I have two such praise files, one in hard copy format for written notes, and one in electronic format for positive e-mails that I have received. I cannot stress strongly enough how valuable these praise files can be. They can help you stay energized and positive about the important work you are doing, and you ARE doing important work! Just as you recognize and compliment others on their work, do the same for yourself. Both you and your teen customers will reap the benefits of this self-recognition.

WEB RESOURCES

American Library Association (ALA): http://www.ala.org—the national professional library organization for library staff in all positions working in any area of library services; it includes divisions such as the PLA and YALSA.

Bibliographic Center for Research: http://www.bcr.org—a multistate library cooperative that serves the library community by providing library and information services, training, and resources.

Teenlibrarian.com: http://www.teenlibrarian.com/—described as an online "community" for those who work with young adults/teens in the library, this site provides news, resources, links, career information, and a portal to many other Web sites and discussion lists.

WebJunction: http://webjunction.org—an online learning community for library staff, this site provides resources, online courses, and information for managing the library and taking advantage of professional growth opportunities.

BIBLIOGRAPHY

Alessio, Amy J., and Kimberly A. Patton. *A Year of Programs for Teens.* Chicago: American Library Association, 2007.

Begley, Sharon, Pat Wingert, Hope White Scott, Ana Figueroa, Devin Gordon, Susannah Meadows, and Michael Cronin. "A World of Their Own." *Newsweek,* May 8, 2000, 53–56.

Benedetti, Angelina. "Crossing Over: A Materials Selector Looks at Adult Books for Teen Readers." *School Library Journal,* June 2004.

Brehm-Heeger, Paula. "Keeping Up with the New." *School Library Journal,* March 2006, 46.

Cox, Michael. "Teen Behavior, Brain Development, and Beating the Boredom Barrage" Lecture, Colorado Association of Libraries Conference, Denver, Colorado, November 10, 2006.

Eisenberg, Michael, and Bob Berkowitz. *Information Problem-Solving: The Big6 Skills Approach to Library and Information Skills Instruction.* Norwood, NJ: Ablex Publishing Corporation, 1990.

Gorman, Michele. "The 'Terrible Teens.'" *School Library Journal,* June 2006, 34.

Herald, Diana Tixier. *Teen Genreflecting: A Guide to Reading Interests.* 2nd ed. Westport, CT: Libraries Unlimited, 2003.

Honnold, RoseMary. *101 + Teen Programs That Work.* New York: Neal-Schuman Publishers, 2003.

Jones, Jami Biles. *Helping Teens Cope: Resources for School Library Media Specialists and Other Youth Workers.* Worthington, OH: Linworth Publishing, 2003.

Jones, Patrick. *Connecting Young Adults and Libraries: A How-To-Do-It Manual.* New York: Neal-Schuman Publishers, 1992.

Libraries Unlimited. *Genreflecting: Genres.* http://www.genreflecting.com/Genres.html#1. Westport, CT: Libraries Unlimited, 2004.

Libretto, Ellen V., and Catherine Barr. *High/Low Handbook: Best Books and Web Sites for Reluctant Teen Readers.* 4th ed. Westport, CT: Libraries Unlimited, 2002.

Management of Reference Committee, Reference Services Section, Reference and User Services Association (RUSA). "RUSA Guidelines: Guidelines for Behavioral Performance of Reference and Information Service Providers." *Reference User Services Quarterly* 44, no. 21 (Fall 2004).

Public Broadcasting System. "Frontline: Inside the Teenage Brain." http://www.pbs.org/wgbh/pages/frontline/shows/teenbrain/. Chicago, IL: WGBH Educational Foundation, 2002.

Spokane Public Libraries. *Collection Development Policy: Spokane Public Library.* Adopted by the Spokane Public Library Board of Trustees, November 19, 2003. Policy Notebook Document #40.1. Spokane, WA: Spokane Public Library Board of Trustees, 2003.

Taney, Kimberly Bolan. *Teen Spaces: The Step-by-Step Library Makeover.* Chicago: American Library Association, 2003.

U.S. Census Bureau. *Census 2000.* Washington, DC: United States Census Bureau, October 31, 2001.

Vaillancourt, Renee J. *Bare Bones Young Adult Services: Tips for Public Library Generalists.* Chicago: American Library Association, 2000.

INDEX

ABOUT THE AUTHOR

DONNA P. MILLER, library media coordinator for the Mesa County Valley School District #51, in Grand Junction, Colorado, has more than 20 years of library experience in schools and public libraries. She has an MLS from the University of North Texas. Miller has served as a consultant for libraries and other organizations and is a frequent presenter at regional and state library conferences. She serves on the board of the Colorado Association of Libraries and is a member of the ALA/CBC Joint Committee. Miller has coauthored two books, *Developing an Integrated Library Program* with J. Anderson, and *Day by Day: Professional Journaling for Library Media Specialists* with K. Larsen, and she is the author of *The Standards-Based Integrated Library*.

Recent Titles in
Libraries Unlimited's Crash C

Crash Course in Children's Services
Penny Peck

Crash Course in Storytelling
Kendall Haven and MaryGay Ducey

Crash Course in Web Design for Libraries
Charles P. Rubenstein

Crash Course in Marketing for Libraries
Susan Webreck Alman

Crash Course in Collection Development
Wayne Disher

Crash Course in Library Supervision: Meeting the Key F
Dennis C. Tucker and Shelley Elizabeth Mosley

Crash Course in Library Gift Programs: The Reluctant Cura
Caring for Archives, Books, and Artifacts in a Library Settin
Ann Roberts

Reference Book Count

before you shelve this book, please list today's date below.